The Insider's Guide

to a Career in

Book Publishing

The Insider's Guide to a Career in Book Publishing

Carin Siegfried

Chickadee Books

Charlotte, North Carolina

WWW.CSEDITORIAL.COM

BOOK DESIGN BY DIANA WADE.

ISBN 978-0-9853362-5-7

FIRST EDITION: JUNE 2014

for Jordan and Betsy, my cheerleaders

The Insider's Guide to a Career in Book Publishing

Contents

Introduction

So you want to work in publishing? Many people dream of collaborating with famous authors, discovering the next J. K. Rowling or Ernest Hemingway. I have worked on many different sides of the industry, from editing manuscripts to selling and buying books, led workshops for writers, and given talks to and mentored college students on how to get a job in the industry. In this book I am going to share what I've learned to help you pursue a successful career in publishing.

Publishing is a hard industry to break into, and the first few years will involve a lot of work for very little pay. I am not trying to discourage you— quite the contrary in fact—this book will give you the information you need to enter the world of books with eyes wide open. The book industry is a rewarding and fascinating career path. There are a lot of benefits. For instance, I get a lot of free books, often before they're published, and have met a few celebrities (such as Michael Palin of Monty Python and Darryl McDaniels of Run-DMC). But most important to me is knowing every day that the work that I do helps put books in people's hands and helps make authors' dreams come true.

The vast majority of people who think about going into publishing want to be editors, which is the path with the least pay and most work (at least in the beginning). A big reason why everyone wants to be an editor initially is that they're unaware of the other career options within publishing. This book takes you through all the major departments of a publishing house and explains the advantages and disadvantages of each. Please don't skip ahead just because you're sure you want to be in editorial; you might miss a career option that is right for you.

I have had a long and broad career in the book industry, ranging across three states, in a variety of departments at several companies. Having had first-hand experience in many of these jobs, I'll give you the inside scoop on what you may like or dislike about various positions. People will tell you that you need to decide what you're going to do with the rest of your life before you're twenty, and if you don't, your life is ruined. Bah! I didn't know what to do career-wise for a long time. Yes, I had experience working in bookstores and libraries, so you'd think I'd be able to see a trend on my résumé, but I didn't. I did flirt with the idea of being an editor, but I was terrified of moving to New York and had no idea what the other options were or even that there were other options! I went to a career counselor three years after graduation to take a series of interest inventories and other career tests. The counselor told me I should be a lawyer. I asked if "editor" was even one of the options on their tests, and she said no.

I was also reluctant to pursue my book publishing dream because people told me that since I didn't start out as an editorial assistant right after graduation, I was always going to be behind and would never catch up. Well, this isn't a race. In fact, I definitely did catch up, and in some ways my peripatetic career has helped me surpass people who took more linear paths. While jumping from department to department isn't for everyone, it helped me more than it hurt, because it gave me a lot of additional knowledge. Thanks to my editorial experience, in my sales job I was able to explain why reprints (especially color) take so long. Thanks to my buying experience, I was able to write the best tip sheets as an editor, and I showed the rest of my imprint what parts of the tip sheets were crucial and explained how they were used and what buyers find useful. Thanks to my bookselling experience, I knew what readers were looking for and why, and what they didn't like as well.

So if you're not sure what to do, if you're already out of school and thinking about changing tracks, if you're already in the book business but want to switch to another area, go for it. If you look for the overlaps, you will see how the knowledge you'll bring to your new arena can give you a boost.

While I've tried to give a broad description of each job and its responsibilities, peoples' experiences will vary, depending upon the house, the editor-in-chief's style, your particular boss, and so on.

Note: This book contains a lot of industry-specific lingo, so if you run across an unfamiliar word (or a familiar word used in an unfamiliar way), please check the glossary at the back. These words appear in the text in a `different font`. In the print edition, an underlined word or phrase indicates a URL is listed in the back of the book under "Resources."

Part I

The Jobs of Publishing

There are numerous jobs in publishing. Editorial is only a small part of the process. Other positions may better fit different personalities.

Chapter 1

Literary Agent

Agenting is closest to what people have in mind when they think of an editor's job, though the job flies below most people's radar. As an agent, you find the manuscript, edit it, send it out to the right editors, hopefully get a sale, and then you've helped launch an author's career. Eventually, you can move away from New York City if you'd like. Many agents end up working for themselves and starting their own agencies.

Agents hopefully will have a lifetime relationship with their authors/clients. Unlike editors, their loyalties aren't nearly as torn between the publishing house and the author, as they help authors navigate the complicated publishing process. While they do need to be careful of their relationship with the publishing house if they want to sell more projects to the publisher in the future, they can be strong advocates for their authors on issues like book jackets and publicity plans. They hunt for new and promising writers, read lots of query letters, and serve as the ultimate matchmakers, trying to pair the right author with the right editor. If the idea of discovering new writers thrills you, as does nurturing a career and a relationship over time, then agenting may be your thing. Agents scour obscure literary journals, go to writers' conventions, contact guests from TV and radio shows, and read manuscripts, including `slush`. Some agents specialize in particular genres, such as mysteries or romance, while others represent a broader range of both fiction and nonfiction, although they likely still have a few genres they prefer to avoid.

Agents need to have good relationships with editors. They meet with them for lunch or drinks (editors pay!) and take notes about what types of books editors are acquiring and what they want to buy. Agents need to research publishing houses so they know which houses publish what types of books well. Those houses will have more and better contacts to publicize books in those genres than if they publish a `one-off`. Agents get to know which editors are hands-on and like to edit with a fine-tooth comb, as opposed to editors who are all about the hunt and need manuscripts that are ready to go to production. When an agent submits a manuscript to an editor, the personality of an editor matters, as does their position in the house and their influence to get promotion and publicity for their books.

Hands-on agents edit the manuscript multiple times. Just like you should never send a first draft of a résumé out in a job search, an agent wouldn't submit a manuscript until it's as near perfect as they and the author can get it. Agents hope it's already in excellent shape when they get it, as they have a lot on their plates already.

Agents negotiate contracts. That shouldn't scare you; you learn negotiation from senior agents over time, and larger agencies tend to have boilerplate contracts on file for the large publishing houses. But this is an area where an agent does help her author get a good deal, a much better deal than the author could get on his own. Often the agent will request to retain certain rights, such as theatrical or foreign. Sometimes those rights can make an enormous amount of money. Who would have thought that a musical based on a retelling of an old fairy tale (*Wicked* by Gregory Maguire) would end up raking in billions? Selling the `subsidiary rights` can help to promote the book in the case of first and second serial, and can also persuade the publishing house to put more money and marketing power behind the promotion of a book when they see that it has been sold in multiple countries. Those sales can really be your author's bread and butter and allow him the freedom to keep writing and pay the rent.

Agents hold the author's hand. They explain the whole publishing process to their clients, about what to expect and when, so the author can set aside time for certain tasks like checking over the copyedited manuscript and reviewing the jacket copy. They run interference for the author when an unsatisfactory cover or publicity plan is presented. They help prep authors for appearances and try to place short pieces in magazines to publish around the same time as the book.

Agents get royalty checks and pay them out to the authors (twice annually in March and October). They work with authors on their next book ideas and strategize over the timing of when to present that proposal to a publisher. They negotiate to get the e-book rights back in the mix if the initial publisher

How accurately is publishing portrayed in novels and movies?

For those of you who still want more information about what it is like to work in publishing, I thought I'd put together a reading list. A friend once begged me to read *The Other Side of the Story* by Marian Keyes. She wanted to know if I thought this story of a literary agent really rang true to someone who knows what that world is like. I thought it was actually pretty accurate as far as that was concerned. And it reminded me of a couple of other books: *The Frog King* by Adam Davies and *As Long As She Needs Me* by Nicholas Weinstock.

Both of these stories were interesting in that they did really show people being more of a personal assistant than an editorial assistant, which was also my experience. I found it noteworthy that they were both written by and star men, although the majority of editorial assistants (and editors) are female. Even though their plots don't revolve around publishing, I thought they were both representative enough about the industry. For more books about publishing, see Chapter 17.

declines to put out an e-book edition. They remind authors of upcoming deadlines.

And they are always looking for marketable new clients, which means reading query letters and manuscripts (sometimes numbering in the thousands per year) and writing tons of rejection letters. (Well, hopefully. Not all agents do rejections anymore, adopting the policy of "no news means no," but it is the polite thing to do.) Longevity is a characteristic of the relationship between an agent and an author, something that's often missing for editors in publishing houses. On average, publishing house editors move every three years, but authors stay with the house. Editors leave authors behind when they pursue a new job. But as an agent, for the most part you get to take authors with you if you change agencies or branch out on your own. Agencies, like publishers, range in size from small boutique offices, such as the Joy Harris Literary Agency or Writers' Representatives, to the massive behemoths of William Morris and ICM.

The entry-level position here is being an agent's assistant. Generally you would be an assistant for one to two years before beginning to acquire your own clients. At a smaller agency, you don't always have to wait for an opening in order to move up. If an agency is open to submissions, as opposed to only working with existing clients or only taking submissions on referral, it's easier for a junior agent to take on new clients. Often a junior agent will inherit authors from agents who have left the industry or retired, so you don't always have to start your own list from scratch (although those authors will not all be ones you would have chosen yourself). As an assistant you will be getting a salary (on par with editorial assistants, around $30,000 yearly), and the first few years that you represent clients, you likely will be paid an annual bonus instead of a commission. The year you transition from a salary to a full commission is a difficult one, and not everyone can do it comfortably. It isn't uncommon for an agent to go through a year with no income during that transition. When this happens varies quite a bit from agency to agency, and some agents make the transition only when they go out on their own. After the transition, your pay will be a percentage of your clients' royalties, which means the bulk of your income will come twice a year. Throughout the year there are small checks, such as for an advance payout upon the signing of a contract for a new book, and again when the author delivers the contract, and when the book is published. But those aren't substantial, so you will need to be very good at budgeting your personal expenses.

One thing to be aware of in the agency world is that some are scams. Any agency that charges fees instead of (or in addition to) a royalty is generally considered a scam within the industry, and reputable publishing houses won't deal with them. Preditors & Editors is a good source of information on which agencies to avoid. Yes, it is geared toward authors, but job seekers should absolutely stay away from those agencies, too. You don't want to be associated with an agency with a bad reputation.

For more information on what agents do daily, check out a few blogs. Miss Snark was a wonderful blog that is sadly no more, but all the archives are still available. BookEnds and Nathan Bransford have great blogs. Look for "A Day in the Life" posts on agency blogs. Jessica at BookEnds posted a compilation of interview questions she is asked repeatedly, and they're pretty much all about having a career as an agent.

Chapter 2

Editor

B ecoming an editor is usually a person's dream job in the publishing industry, but it's a long road to get there. In editorial, you start out as an editorial assistant, with an average starting salary of $29,000 for the smaller publishing houses to $35,000 for midsize houses. Editorial pays the least and promotes the slowest of all jobs in publishing. It's probably your dream job right now, but it's nowhere near as glamorous as you imagine.

After paying your dues as an editorial assistant, you get promoted to assistant editor, then associate editor. All three of these positions cover a lot of the same ground—only the degree varies. You don't get an office or get out of answering someone else's phone until you have been associate editor for a while, or even until you get promoted to editor.

When starting as an assistant, whom you report to is important. The higher up in the company they are, the more you'll learn about the industry, but the less freedom you'll have and the less editorial experience you'll get, as you'll be more of a personal assistant. Younger editors, while less influential, remember better what it was like to be an assistant, can be better mentors, and likely will give you more responsibility earlier. But fewer managers at the company will know who you are.

An editorial assistant:

- Answers phones.

- Opens and sorts mail.

- Makes lunch reservations.

- Waters plants.

- Maintains their boss's schedule.

- Types their boss's rejection letters (thanks to Outlook, you can send e-mails on behalf of your boss from your own desk).

- Maintains and updates their boss's submission database.

- Fills out deal sheets for their boss and sends them to the appropriate departments.

- Fills out check request forms.

- Sends out contracts.

- Sends Author Questionnaires to authors; ensures they are returned.

- Attends Editorial, Art, and Launch meetings (preparing any materials that might be necessary in advance, such as author sales history).

- Makes copies of manuscripts; routes them to readers.

- Makes files for new books, being sure appropriate material is in the file.

So far, these duties may not be what you expected, perhaps? Sounds like a personal assistant, not a junior editor, right? Well, that is the bulk of the job. And it can be worse. One assistant I knew had to get her boss's furs out of storage every fall and put them back in the spring. I had to make my boss's personal bank deposits and reserve limos to the airport for him. Luckily the days of assistants having to do their boss's expense reports are generally past, as those are online now. That's good, because the first expense report I submitted after my boss spent three weeks in London was for $25,000. Yes, that was more than my annual salary, thanks for asking! For me it was really demoralizing.

My favorite of the numerous tasks at my publishing house was the "Meeting meeting." That's no typo. Three times a year there would be a meeting of all the department heads' assistants where we'd go through the master schedule for the upcoming season of publications, and we'd adjust the master schedule to be sure all the people who needed to be at the meetings didn't have any conflicts. At least we got free doughnuts!

You do get to work on some books, but not doing actual editing, at least at first. You will be assigned between four and twelve books a season. (In publishing there usually are three seasons a year in adult publishing and two in children's.) The first books you'll be assigned will be imports, foreign offsets, and paperback reprints: all of which require no editing. If your boss does assign you a domestic manuscript, she will be doing the editing, and you'll be doing the grunt work. That includes:

- Writing the flap copy or back copy.

- Writing the catalog copy.

- Writing the sales tip sheets.

- Mailing out copyedited manuscripts to authors, ensuring they are returned on time, returning them to production (this may be done electronically at some publishing houses now).

- Making sure the boss signs off on jacket mechanicals and they are returned to art quickly.

- Mailing out galley with letters for prepublication blurb.

- Sending out an author's contract copies of his finished book.

You will be at the assistant job from one to three years before acquiring your own manuscripts. Meanwhile, you will need to be making agent contacts. Be super nice to the agents (and agents' assistants) you talk with on the phone. They might end up liking you more than your boss and start sending you things, because you actually follow up and keep your word. Research which agents you want to meet. Start off with a list of books you wish you'd published, and find out who agented those. Google is your friend, as is Publishers Marketplace. Once your boss has given you the okay (and you have an expense account), you will then cold e-mail agents and ask them out to lunch or drinks, then spend the hour talking about what kinds of books you hope to buy. Then when those manuscripts start to come in, you will read them and reject most of them. There are gems occasionally, but you have to sift through a lot of dross to get to them.

When you find a book you like, you'll go tell your boss. She will ask a few other people to read it (maybe someone in sales or marketing). If those reports come back positive, she will quiz you about a few things, such as how you think this will sell. How many would you print? You will have already told your boss if the author has a platform, an audience, a hook, or media contacts. If you're lucky your boss will say, "Okay, you can buy this. Offer them ten thousand dollars for world rights." Alternately you may have to take the project in front of the editorial board, which might be thirty people or more, and then on to the publisher board. Other editors and people from marketing, publicity, and sales will ask innumerable questions, poke holes in your assertions about why the book works, and confront you with similar titles that may have already saturated the marketplace. You will need to defend your book and why it's a good idea. If you are successful in your presentation and convince the boards, you will then have the happiest and most nerve-wracking day of your life. Now you will need to call the agent and negotiate the contract, which can be tricky if they want more money, and trickier if they are going to auction. You will worry the author will turn out to be high-maintenance. And most of all, you will be terrified that the book will fail and not sell, as that's true more often than not. In 2007 Jonathan Karp, publisher of Twelve at Hachette, said that publishing is a corporate form of legalized gambling. Seven out of eight books fail in hardcover. You can't be easily discouraged in this field. But keep in mind the future. The publisher of Grove/Atlantic, Morgan Entrekin, famously has a policy that anyone can buy a book, and if it works you can buy another. It sounds great, but the unspoken corollary is if your book doesn't sell, you'll have an uphill battle to acquire your second book.

Are you perhaps again wondering, where is all the editing? The cold, hard fact is that even once you become an editor, you don't spend your days at work revising manuscripts. Editors are busy doing other things at work, so all the reading and editing is done at home, in their spare time. Being an editor means having a never-ending pile of homework for the rest of your life.

What is editing? When editing a manuscript, an editor isn't looking for issues with grammar or punctuation; that's for the copyeditor (see **chapter 5**). Editors look for larger things: characterization, plot, tone, consistency, timing, pacing. It's great to also be able to do a line edit, in which you do look at word choice and phrasing, but these days, not all editors have the time to go into that level of editing. In rare cases, if a book is otherwise great but needs a lot of editing that an editor just can't do, they might hire an independent editor to complete the editing or suggest to the author that they should do that. The editor might make a conditional offer of publication, depending on how the manuscript reads after the revision. Alternatively, at times an editor needs to remind an author that their contract can be cancelled if their manuscript is deemed unsatisfactory.

An editor needs to be extremely diplomatic and often spends her days putting out fires. For example, when your author calls to say her publicist isn't returning her calls, you need to call the publicist and convince them to do that. When the art designer designs a jacket that—while beautiful—just isn't right for the book, you need to explain that to him in a way that doesn't

The slush pile

The first books I was assigned to work on as an editorial assistant were a one-thousand-page biography of Yeltsin, a British cozy mystery, a travel book about a remote Greek island, and a sweet historical novel about farm girls in England during WWII. Diverse, yes. My cup of tea, no. This is pretty common. You won't always like the books you're assigned to work on, but that's not a terrible thing, as it will allow for more impartiality.

After months of the basics, while your colleagues and bosses find out your opinions on books and whether you've got your head screwed on straight, after giving a ton of editorial reports, you'll get your first crack at something that finally seems "editorial": the Slush Pile.

The Slush Pile is a sometimes well-managed, other times overgrown pile of unsolicited (unagented) manuscripts that have come through the mail (and e-mail) unrequested. The authors ought to be submitting to agents, not to major publishers, and it's astonishing how many of them submit books that are patently wrong for the publishing house. A friend

cause him to go cry (they're sensitive) and also doesn't result in him purposefully designing a bad jacket to try to force you to accept the first jacket. Other times, everyone will love the jacket, from marketing to sales to your boss to her boss to his boss. But your author will hate it. She will call you crying (they're sensitive), swearing that this cover will ruin the book and she won't be able to promote it in good conscience. You will have to convince her to do so, because that jacket just isn't getting redone.

Editors talk to marketing and sales and try to convince them to promote their books among the hundreds they are dealing with, although there's no budget for it and no platform and no publicity. They persuade an author (who got into this line of work because she isn't a "people person" and she likes to sit home alone with her computer) that she needs to call local bookstores and set up events, call her alumni office, and will need to actually do readings (some might panic over this prospect). And then of course, the editor needs to convince her author to happily make the editorial changes you think are crucial. The best editors convince her that those changes are what she intended all along and are her ideas.

Editors must be very broadly read. While reading a thousand manuscript pages a week, you have to keep up with reading published books from other houses. You need to know what's going on in the marketplace (which sometimes means reading mega best sellers, even though you know you won't like them, but the public does). Also, when you've read several dozen horrible manuscripts, a mediocre one looks fantastic in comparison. So you need to keep up your outside reading in order to keep your standards high. You need a critical eye and the ability to trust your own judgment.

While all this extra work is added to your plate, the previous duties are still part of your job description. An editor spends most of her day on paperwork and e-mail or in meetings. After all, reviews need to be sent out, books need to be submitted for appropriate awards, sales reports need to be run, print runs need to be ordered, books need to be scheduled, copyedits need to be reviewed. It's a tough, unglamorous job. Luckily for us readers, there are a lot of dedicated, talented editors out there. But being an editor isn't for everyone. Many people who think they want to be an editor would be better off as an agent. Reread that section if you want to discover unknown authors, have lifelong relationships with authors, and help craft authors' careers.

of mine worked at a house that only published children's books. More than half of their slush pile was adult novels. Many of the bigger houses have a no-unsolicited-manuscripts policy, so the slush is immediately recycled or deleted, but not all publishers have this cutoff. And a lot of submissions will come in electronically these days, so rejections can be painless. If you have the time, you are probably welcome to look through the slush pile. But most slush submissions are barely glanced at while their SASEs are stuffed with form rejection letters. Once in a blue moon something decent will come through the slush pile. It is actually where I found my first acquisition.

My personal favorite slush submission ever was from a man who wanted to write the definitive biography of JFK Jr., which he felt he was uniquely positioned to write as he used to summer with JFK Jr. in Kentucky (red flag, anyone?), he knew where the illegitimate children were hidden, and had firsthand knowledge that JFK Jr. was gay. The return address was for a prison!

Chapter 3

Subsidiary Rights Representative

I bet you've never heard of subsidiary rights, but it's an important way to maximize the sales from a book. Subsidiary rights reps sell audio rights, large-print rights, foreign rights, film rights, reprint rights, and so on. The people selling foreign rights get to travel internationally several times a year, usually attending the Frankfurt, London, and Bologna book fairs. It can be an even more important and exciting job on the children's side, where the licensing of characters (for toys, cereal boxes, and TV shows) is much more likely than in the adult world.

Reprint rights can help get the public's attention for a book, such as when an excerpt is printed in *Vanity Fair* or *U.S. News and World Report*. Any foreign rights sale goes a long way toward the bottom line and can make the difference between a book being profitable or not. Foreign sales also get the attention of American booksellers, who are more likely to give a book a chance if it's been picked up in multiple countries. That vote of confidence justifies the bookstore buyer purchasing more copies and planning a more prominent display. The publicist can also use that information to get more reviews.

In children's publishing, character licensing promotes brand development and can drive kids to pick up books. It can be easy to trash the commercialization of children's literature, but every time someone buys a *Fancy Nancy* lunch box or a set of *Pinkalicious* barrettes, an author gets another check with which to pay her mortgage! And it's never good to tar everything with a wide brush—after all, tons of respected classics are licensed widely, from *Winnie-the-Pooh* to *Paddington Bear* to *The Very Hungry Caterpillar*. Licenses allow authors and illustrators to quit their day jobs and really concentrate on their craft.

This job has a more relaxed atmosphere than editorial. But it does take patience and persistence and a matchmaking state of mind. And in this area, you have very little interaction with authors. But that can be a plus. Authors aren't always the easiest people to deal with (ah, artists!).

Subrights is a mix of sales and agenting. Like an agent, the subrights representative tries to send out a novel to the foreign editors most likely to see the promise and potential. Naturally, there is selling involved and some contracts, but mostly boilerplate, so don't let that scare you off. It can be a very creative position as well. (I wonder who first thought of making Kraft Macaroni & Cheese into shapes, such as SpongeBob SquarePants?) Stores sell everything from *Hunger Games*–inspired nail polish and flip-flops to *Harry Potter* "Bertie Botts" candy, and there are crazier licensed products out there. (In fact, some items licensed from *Twilight* and *Fifty Shades of Grey* are X-rated!)

Usually the publisher and an author's agent split the rights sales. So the publisher might get English-language rights while the agent retains foreign language. But they often work cooperatively, as proceeds are split between the publisher and author (and author's agent). In this example the publisher would work to sell off the Canadian, UK, and Australian/New Zealand rights. They can also sell English-language books in India, Singapore, South Africa, and for European export.

The markets for both large-print and audio have been growing of late. Audio is mostly due to the success of the iPod and iPhone, as well as lengthening work commutes. Large-print is very directly tied to the aging of baby boomers, although large-print books are also perfect for reading on the treadmill.

It's not that frequent that books get turned into movies or TV shows or plays (mostly these rights are held by the agent), but it does happen sometimes, such as with HBO's *True Blood*. This is also the department someone who wants to reprint an essay or a short story in an anthology or textbook would contact. But really, aren't the key chains, bobbleheads, and board games the real fun in this arena? And yes, literary agencies also employ subrights reps; usually they have partnerships with a few foreign agencies, and they might also have a partner in Hollywood to handle theatrical and other performance rights.

The department is very small. Even in the biggest publishing houses it might consist of only two or three people, one of whom is an assistant. Because it's so small, the assistant does get to see a lot of what goes on and has a lot of managing responsibilities, particularly when the reps are traveling.

Chapter 4

Production Editor and Production Manager

The production editor and managing editor, who shepherd the project from manuscript to printed book, are the unsung heroes of publishing. The managing editorial department is vital to the publication of a book. This job is ideal for highly organized, efficient people who enjoy learning the finer points of grammar and language, and who may find the prospect of interacting with agents and authors and dealing with contracts and pitches off-putting. The average starting salary for a managing editorial assistant (or assistant to the managing editor) is $28,000 to $30,000.

Sometimes newbies to the publishing industry see the title "production editor" but only the word "editor" makes an impact. They can be quite surprised to find that the job actually entails behind-the-scenes work—which also means out-of-the-crossfire work—and it pays reasonably well and usually doesn't involve the same type of editorial homework, such as reading proposals or meeting with agents or potential authors.

In the months leading up to the transmittal, the editor has discussed an estimated page count, trim size, and season or month of publication with the managing editor. After an editor and author have worked on a manuscript to their mutual satisfaction, the manuscript is transmitted to the managing ed department. The managing editor will assign the book to a production editor, who then works with a text or interior designer and a production manager. The production editor is the point person between the production and design departments and editorial. The production manager is the coordinator between production and the printers and warehouses and shippers.

Publishing houses divide these jobs differently and there can be overlap, so you may find differences from my descriptions. Some houses also employ exclusively digital production editors who coordinate e-book publishing, including formatting, digital rights management (DRM), layout conversions, and metadata compilation, all of which can be very complicated for backlist titles (books published more than a couple of years ago) that were originally formatted on film, not digitally, and need to be converted. Houses without a dedicated digital production editor rely on their production editors to handle the e-book coordination as well.

The Role of a Production Editor:

The managing editor often makes the production schedule for the manuscript, and will also make the jacket routing schedule, working in conjunction with the production editor to ensure the schedules stay on track.

Production editors sometimes make up the production schedule on their own or collaborate with the design and production departments to create a production schedule, based on when a book needs to be finalized before being sent to the printer. The schedule is distributed, maintained—or reevaluated as the book moves through production—and followed-up on. A production editor works with the editor to ensure all parts of the manuscript have been transmitted; if any elements, such as a dedication or the acknowledgments, are missing, the production editor marks those as "to come" (or TK) and coordinates with the editor on a due date.

The production editor contracts with a copyeditor and sends the manuscript—either on paper, still a common method with older authors and at smaller publishing houses, or in a Word document, to be reviewed using Track Changes—out for copyediting. When the copyeditor returns the manuscript (usually in about three weeks), the production editor sends it to the editor, who passes it to the author for review. When it's returned from the author (they normally have two weeks to review), the production editor goes over the copyeditor's and author's changes to be sure nothing unusual was added or omitted and that all queries were addressed, checks to make sure all pages are still included (if the copyedit was done on paper), and so on. One of the production editor's most important jobs at this stage is to "clean up" the manuscript: in other words, to be sure that all the changes requested have been input correctly, that formatting is clear, and that if an element is missing, an approximate page count has been assigned (e.g., three pages for an author's note).

Meanwhile, during the copyediting stage and author review, the interior designer has come up with a design concept (or "page layout") that has been approved by the editor and author. The production editor now sends the copyedited manuscript to be typeset by a compositor. While the manuscript is being typeset, the production editor (or editorial assistant, at some imprints) applies for the copyright and Library of Congress cataloging-in-publication (CIP) data.

The compositor returns the typeset files (or "page proofs") anywhere from three to four weeks later, after which the production editor sends them off to be proofread. In addition to looking for typos and story inconsistencies, the proofreaders check all the running heads for consistency, spacing, and accuracy, and also check the page numbers. They watch for "ladders," "stacks," and "bad breaks" in hyphenated words. In this job it can sometimes be easier to work on books you don't like, as getting caught up in reading makes it easy to miss the details.

A heavily designed book with photos, captions, sidebars, footnotes, a glossary, etc., will be a very involved job for the production editor. Most publishing houses do a second proofread before the pages are ready to be printed. If necessary, the production editor will send the page proofs off to an indexer and coordinate the index, which is ideally done at the last minute, after every other step before printing. The production editor makes sure the jacket designers stay on schedule and copyedits the jacket/flap copy.

All along the way, a production editor does spot-checks to make sure the freelancers are doing their jobs correctly, using the appropriate house style guide, and working according to guidelines. If any new book material comes in after the copyedit, the production editor handles copyediting that. So while you do not do a ton of copyediting and proofreading, you need to be familiar with those jobs and with *The Chicago Manual of Style*.

The Role of a Production Manager:
This person is responsible for production of final proofs and print-ready / web-ready PDFs and plates. The production manager handles print orders, maintains records, and conducts bidding and consultation with printers. She serves as the primary liaison with domestic and international fulfillment houses, directs book orders to the appropriate distributor, and approves all invoices related to production and passes them on for payment. She selects the paper and the casing for hardcover books.

Once the production department has sent off the book to the printer, the book is out of the publisher's hands. The printer's support reps price out the job for the publisher's production team and route the files to the appropriate departments. Books are printed on giant pages with sixteen-page sheets (they look like eight, but the other eight are on the back). For small or very short-notice printing, a short-run printer for POD (print on demand) might be used instead. Some publishers are also using POD for their older backlist titles that don't sell enough to merit another full printing of two thousand copies but whose sales haven't yet dropped off to the point where the publisher declares the book out of print or out of stock indefinitely.

Production and managing editorial make sure a book is copyedited, fact-checked, and proofread, and that everything goes smoothly. The ultimate behind-the-scenes workers, they deal with the printers, make sure everything's on schedule, and are the last line of defense against typos. They coordinate the jacket production with art, the interior with design, and the manuscript with editorial. They truly are in charge of the production.

Chapter 5

Copyeditor and Proofreader

Copyeditors and proofreaders are detail-oriented people who check that everything is spelled correctly and that the grammar used is appropriate. They usually work freelance, outside of publishing houses, though some imprints employ full-time in-house copyeditors. Even if you consider yourself to be a careful reader, you definitely need to take at least one or two classes to train to properly do this job. The work can be tedious, and it can be difficult to keep yourself fully employed, but you can have a lot more freedom working for yourself.

When I was an editor at St. Martin's Press, 90 percent of people I met outside of the industry assumed I would be fixing spelling and punctuation. I would roll my eyes and smile, and explain for the hundredth time, no, that's a completely different and very specialized job.

Working freelance can be nerve-wracking: No corporate health insurance. No vacation days. But on the other hand—no boss. No office. No nine-to-five grind. You can work when you need to, and not work when you don't. You can live somewhere that is not New York City. The freedom and flexibility can be really liberating. To break into this career, you need to network with managing editors and production editors. Send out cold e-mails. Network in whatever copyediting classes you take, including asking the professor for help connecting with publishing insiders.

Copyediting or proofreading novels and narrative nonfiction (memoirs) pays the least. If you have specialized knowledge in technical, medical, or scientific subjects, you can charge much, much more. The same goes for projects like heavily researched history books. The projects are more work, but the pay rate is related to supply. Not as many copyeditors and proofreaders can work on more obscure or more technical subject matter. Of course, there also aren't a ton of those types of books published each year, so someone working on general fiction will have an easier time obtaining very steady work.

Most copyeditors are paid by the hour. Thirty dollars an hour is a good benchmark for a standard manuscript, with specialists earning thirty-five to one hundred dollars an hour. Obviously, there is wide range. Payment is sometimes by the word, and a clean eighty-thousand-word manuscript can pay anywhere from $650 to $800. A heavy copyedit on a sloppy manuscript that needs a lot of work can pay between 50 to 250 percent more.

The Role of a Copyeditor:

Copyeditors check a number of aspects in a manuscript: grammar, punctuation, accuracy of dates (a character can't go to a Starbucks in 1978 because Starbucks didn't exist then), trademarks (not only do trademarked words all need to be capitalized, but a character cannot order a Grand Slam Breakfast at Waffle House), and style and story consistency. Every publishing house has a style guide, dictating if they prefer to write numbers out—"twenty-one"—or use numerals—"21"—and how various compound words should be handled. The style guide will have a long list of words and examples where the publishing house has made a decision; therefore all of their books will be consistent.

The copyeditor then creates a manuscript-specific style guide, which includes a list of character names, places, and events. Book publishing generally uses *The Chicago Manual of Style* as their style guide of choice, to direct a copyeditor in decisions ranging from serial commas (yes) to excessive hyphenations (no). You will need to have additional reference books to check everything from when bird names are capitalized (when they contain a proper noun, such as Cooper's hawk) to how latitude and longitude are notated (32°16'31") to how to note proper military rankings (General of the Army). A copyeditor will check that foreign-language phrases are accurate, that real place names are spelled correctly, that acronyms are correct and explained the first time they are used if uncommon, and that slang is used consistently. When working on a book series, a master style guide will be created, which will apply to all the books in the series, not just the one in front of you. As a copyeditor, you get noticed only for your mistakes.

Were you born to be a copyeditor?
by Kathleen Cook, Production Editor at Vintage and Anchor at Random House

Here's how you become a good copyeditor and proofreader: read. Everything from classics to current best sellers, *New York Times* articles to celebrity gossip blogs, from literary fiction to memoirs to trashy romance novels. Whatever you do, read.

Copyediting and proofreading require a curiosity for language and grammar and punctuation; if you get a thrill from knowing that it's "minuscule" and not "miniscule" or "hairbreadth" and not "hair's breadth," you may be a natural. By continuing to read, you will learn the different language or structural preferences in certain genres or how sometimes the author's poetic intent supersedes grammatical correctness. There is an art to copyediting; in addition to knowing rule after rule after rule, the more subjects you've read about, the more help you'll be in fine-tuning an author's work. Your goals should be to continue learning about a wide range of subjects and to develop an ear for language.

If you're able, you should consider taking a copyediting or proofreading course. These classes are often offered at night, as part of the continuing education program at colleges and universities. You can also find several reputable programs online; be sure to research online programs carefully. You want the best instruction and advice that you can afford. Classes are often taught by an industry professional, many with fifteen or twenty years' worth of publishing experience. You want to take a class with an instructor who is still currently working in publishing; it is a rapidly changing business, with digital advancements that those outside the industry may not know about.

In a copyediting and proofreading class, you will learn the finer points of these jobs and the common terminology. Being a careful and enthusiastic reader is a wonderful baseline for being a careful copyeditor and proofreader, but many aspiring freelancers believe that's all it takes. As a production editor, I love working with careful readers who take the time to digest the book (even if it's not their favorite subject or author). But I also love freelancers who know all of their responsibilities as a copyeditor and proofreader—such as checking the running heads and page folios on each page—and how to mark errors correctly—like when to label something a widow or an orphan. The publishing industry moves at a quick pace these days; as a new freelancer, you want to be as prepared as possible in order to make the best impression and keep being assigned work.

You'll also make publishing connections in a copyediting and proofreading class. The person sitting to your right may be an associate production editor hoping to brush up on her skills; to your left may be an editor who is interested in doing freelance work in his spare time. Your instructor may be your best bet for getting your foot inside the door; if you impress her in class, she will likely be happy to give you freelance work or put you in contact with other potential clients. Or you can use your new connections when applying for jobs at publishing houses. The industry is a surprisingly small world.

If you're interested in becoming a production editor, you'll want to apply for positions as an assistant to the managing editor (or some variation of that wording). At most imprints, you'll work under the managing editor and also assist the department's production editors. Be prepared to keep track of an extraordinary number of details and to be extremely organized. You'll learn how book schedules are prepared—and how quickly they can go off course. If you're lucky, you'll also work closely with the editorial, design, art, and production departments and have ample opportunity to learn what each department does in their day-to-day operations. (If you're like me, you'll also learn how happy you are not to be an editorial assistant!) Managing editorial assistants who are good at their jobs and proactive about developing their copyediting and proofreading skills can move up quickly to associate production editor and eventually to production editor.

Two resources to consider if you want to learn more about being a copyeditor or proofreader are *The Subversive Copy Editor: Advice from Chicago* (or, *How to Negotiate Good Relationships with Your Writers, Your Colleagues, and Yourself*) by Carol Fisher Saller and *The Copyeditor's Handbook: A Guide for Book Publishing and Corporate Communications* by Amy Einsohn. If the role of a production editor interests you and you want to learn more, seek out internship opportunities or apply to attend a summer publishing course, such as the Columbia Publishing Course offered through Columbia University's journalism school.

Whatever you decide to do, remember my first piece of advice: read everything you can get your hands on. Loving books is not enough: develop a passion for language, for the details. These skills will serve you well no matter where you end up.

The Role of a Proofreader:

A proofreader reads carefully through the typeset pages looking for any typos or errors and anything inconsistent with the style guide. New errors can be introduced in the typesetting and formatting process, which makes proofreading particularly essential. Proofreaders work off of the first-pass pages (the first version of typeset pages printed), and most big publishing houses also do a second proofread on the second- or third-pass pages. The ARCs, or Advance Reader's Copies (used in publicity and sales) usually are printed from the first-pass pages, so they frequently have errors.

Copyeditor versus copy editor

While I was writing this book, Kathleen Cook (who wrote the preceding sidebar) pointed out that *Webster's 11th Collegiate Dictionary* has changed their entry to recommend "copy editor" as two words when used like it is here, as a noun, although it keeps "copyediting" and "copyedit" as one word. I found that confusing and also to not be parallel to "proofreader," which is one word, and was dismayed. My copyeditor then found a contrarian article on *The Subversive Copy Editor Blog*, written by Carol Saller, a senior manuscript editor at the University of Chicago Press, an editor of *The Chicago Manual of Style*, and editor of the *Chicago Manual of Style Online's Q&A*. Someone wrote in, noting that she uses "copy editor" as two words in her book but as one word in her blog. She explained that in her book, while she had been following *Webster's*, this is a word where *CMOS* disagrees and specifically states they prefer one word. She did delete all references to the word from the *CMOS* except four, but this is a perfect example of when there aren't hard-and-fast

When a manuscript is entered into the interior design program, it is no longer a series of words; it is an image, so spell-check programs no longer work. (Not to mention spell-check programs have never worked on homophones.) This means that at this stage, if an author decides to change something, such as a character's name, the change must be made by hand in every instance, as find-and-replace also doesn't work in this program for the same reason.

A lot of what a proofreader does is check the typesetting and the page design. You will be looking to be sure all the page numbers are there, in order, and in the right place. You will check that the chapter headers and running heads are correct. You will check that facing pages are balanced and one isn't accidentally a line shorter or longer than the rest. You will check hyphenations both for accuracy (is that where that word should be hyphenated?) and to be sure they don't go across a page break awkwardly. The proofreader eliminates ladders and stacks, and widows (a line at the top of a page that is not a full-length line) and orphans (when three or fewer characters fall on a line by themselves) when possible.

Proofreaders are the last set of eyes between a typo and the printer, so while on the one hand it isn't a very taxing job (although the books can be boring or complicated), on the other hand it can have pressure. Readers do contact publishing houses about errors in finished books, and those notices go to the production editor to be fixed in a future printing.

Obviously if the production editor notices a lot of errors in books proofread by the same person, he will stop hiring that proofreader. Because the job is less difficult and less time-consuming than copyediting, it doesn't pay as well, about twenty-five dollars an hour, but a full-time freelance proofreader may be able to accept many more projects than someone who only copyedits. In fact, many freelancers do both and switch off between copyediting and proofreading.

rules and when copyeditors have to make judgment calls. Traditional publishers will have a house style guide that should give rulings on controversies like this. In self-publishing, it's an issue for the copyeditor and author to work out.

In my book, I have used "copyeditor," all one word. That's the way I've always done it, I like that it matches with the one-word usage in "copyediting" and "copyedit," and also with the job title "proofreader." (Although I hear the point that one does not write "developmental-editor" or "lineeditor" as all one word, I think that's a specious argument as those are unwieldy and the double "e" in "lineeditor" would be problematic.) The author's preference does trump all style guides, provided her decision is made for a reason and is applied consistently.

Chapter 6

Art Designer and Interior Designer

In adult books the design department creates the interior, while art designs the jacket or cover. The jacket is what the publisher presents to the world, but the interior text is what the actual book consists of. In children's books, these are the same department, as the interior illustrations are often a crucial component to the jacket design as well.

These are both wonderful options for art majors who would like company-sponsored health insurance and a regular paycheck. Both need a background in art, and you must be able to take criticism, be willing to edit your ideas, and understand that books are a collaborative effort.

The average pay for graphic designers working in book publishing is $37,000, but that includes everyone, not just entry-level.

The role of an art designer:

The jacket isn't just the front cover. It includes the back cover, spine, and flaps for a hardcover, and a front, back, and spine for paperbacks. At the beginning of a season the art department will come to editorial for a jacket meeting. All of the books for the upcoming season will be reviewed briefly, with the editor telling the art designer of any particular direction for a given book. They might say, "It needs to look like a big book" (which usually means all big type on the front), or say, "It's a chick-lit novel, but please can it not be pink or yellow, as those colors are so overplayed?" or "This book really appeals to readers of Jodi Picoult, so can we do a design that looks pretty much like her last book?"

Editors might bring in actual copies of book jackets to emulate or inspire a book's design. They should give a brief description of the book, and if there's any important symbolism or talisman that ought to be featured prominently, this would be the time for the editor to mention it. The editor also should convey any of the author's ideas. The designers will get copies of the manuscripts, but given the time frame, if they're able to read the first fifty pages of each book they're assigned, that's a lot. The more direction editorial can give them, the better.

If this is not a debut book, the back cover needs to leave room for blurbs for the author's previous book (or room for blurbs on the paperback of a book that was published in hardcover), but if it is a first book, the designer may need to come up with something more creative for the back cover to obscure that there are no blurbs. The designer needs to leave room for logos, barcodes, pricing, and so on. Spines are sadly often neglected. The wording (title, subtitle, and author) on the front cover needs to be readable. The cover needs to convey the proper tone, feel, and atmosphere for the book.

A jacket designer will need to come up with two to five different design concepts for a jacket, which then need to be approved by the editor, publisher, marketing, and sales, and one will come out as the frontrunner. Sometimes an author will have "jacket consultation" in their contract, which can slow the process down, but that isn't the same as "jacket approval" (which almost no authors have). All of these people will rip the different designs to pieces. An art designer really does need to have a thick skin. While yes, this is art, it has to be legible, appropriate, accurate, and scream, "Buy me!" They might have to rework a design fifteen times. They will get conflicting comments. They work on very tight deadlines. And they have small budgets for most every book. Any special features like a matte cover, spot gloss, a fifth or sixth color (silver, gold), foil, step-backs, or die-cuts add expense. Sometimes a designer will be very clever and manage to squeeze a special feature into their budget, such as matte, by not doing a four-color (cyan, magenta, yellow, and black (CMYK)) jacket. Some really appealing jackets have been done with only two or three colors.

The role of an interior designer:
Meanwhile, the interior designer is also working away. Most people don't notice, but usually in adult books the interior and exterior fonts and designs are completely different (not always of course). They both might appeal to different audiences. And a font that's really cool for the title might really grate after four hundred pages. The interior designer picks the fonts, the chapter headers, where page numbers fall, and if it's a heavily designed book,

they might also work on sidebars, callouts, photo captions, quizzes, quotes, illustrations, maps, table of contents, and so on. For cookbooks, travel books, poetry collections, picture books, and other specialized books there's even more detail work for the interior designer. The interior designer comes up with a layout and style sheet. The book's editor and her boss will sign off on the interior, after consulting the author. The approved design will go with the copyedited manuscript to the compositor for the pages to be typeset.

While the interior designer doesn't have the most glamorous job, it's almost more important, and yet it's lower pressure, without the big meetings full of executives picking the designer's ideas apart. It can have a lot more design elements to it and can make or break a book, especially if not completed in a timely fashion. If a jacket really doesn't work, the publishing house will often redesign it for the paperback, but the interior will stay the same aside from minor copyediting corrections.

If you look up the winners of the AIGA 50 Books/50 Covers competition, you'll see half the winners are for covers, whereas half are for the book itself. A few blogs post about identical or very similar cover images. Stock images are often used nonexclusively so it happens from time to time. Another issue in the jacket design world is the whitewashing of minority characters, which is when characters of color are portrayed as very light-skinned, so much so that they could pass for white, regardless of how they're described in the book. And many readers don't like that more often than not British and American jackets for the same book are different (and the title sometimes is too), causing confusion. But the marketplaces are so different that the look or feel of a British book often just doesn't translate here. (Not to mention the British publishing house might be charging a very steep fee to use their jacket design.)

Another issue that comes up from time to time is the redesign of backlist books. The backlist is what pays the bills, so you want it to sell, sell, sell. Redesigning book covers allows the sales department to resolicit titles to bookstores, reminding bookstores about these books, in the hope that they'll bring in a few more copies, maybe even display a few. A clever redesign of backlist occurred after the popularity of *Twilight*, when classic novels that inspired the author Stephenie Meyer, such as *Wuthering Heights* and *Romeo and Juliet*, were all redesigned with jackets similar in look and feel to the Twilight series.

Chapter 7

Publicist

The second most popular job in publishing after editor is publicist. It's due to a combination of A) applicants having actually heard the word and having a vague idea of what the job entails and B) the quantity of job postings in the department. The latter should scare people. Lots of job postings often means the job lends itself to a high burnout rate. That said, obviously some people are going to love this job and be fantastic at it. And who are those people?

Publicists need to be outgoing, enthusiastic, and good at schmoozing. If you were a social chair at a sorority or a fraternity, this could be the perfect job for you.

A publicist is on the phone constantly, talking to reporters, talk-show management, and radio stations, pitching the books and authors she's been assigned, trying to get them any sort of media attention. She's also talking to authors, agents, and editors to update them. She writes and sends out press releases along with review copies (usually galleys or ARCs) to magazines and newspapers and other media outlets. The press release is really important because sometimes a review or article will include large parts of the release, lifted nearly verbatim.

These days, a publicist is dealing with book bloggers in addition to the usual print reviewers, both industry and trade. Publicists try to get authors reviewed, interviewed, and featured in the media. If she gets an author a spot on radio or TV, she then needs to prep the author and be sure he's ready for the media, which can be time-consuming (authors are not all socially savvy). The success rate of actually getting attention for a book is low, so you can't be easily discouraged.

Publicists go to book launch parties and show tapings, take magazine features editors out for dinner, and occasionally meet celebrities. The high burnout factor with this job tends to result from overwork. A publicist will be assigned anywhere from ten to twenty-five authors a season, and hardly any authors are satisfied with the attention their book receives.

Publicists also need to be familiar with the publishers' entire backlist to utilize the list with major events. For instance, when a volcano erupts, if you have a vulcanologist who wrote a book for your house four years ago, you can pitch him to major newspapers as an expert whom they can interview. A good publicist can pitch almost any nonfiction author and even some fiction authors as an expert on something. Even if you have no experts, if you have a native of the area in question, you can still pitch them to national papers as someone to talk to about the experience of living through one of these traumatic events. The backlist is what actually makes the house money, so when you can do this, it's really important.

When an author goes on a tour, his publicist is his primary contact. At larger publishing houses there's normally one person in the publicity department whose job is to coordinate tours, which entails contacting bookstores, finding out how many copies they need, getting the order placed and expedited and tracked, as well as providing any promotional material to the store beforehand, such as a poster, biography, or photo. Publishers rarely pay for a tour these days, but authors will often self-fund one, particularly to cities where they are from or went to college or lived for a few years and therefore may have a built-in audience. The publicist still needs to be sure that local media is alerted and coordinated, and that the books get there, even when the publisher isn't organizing or paying for the tour.

Publicity can be exciting and fun, but it is also anxiety-ridden because it can make or break a book. Here is an example using a book I edited. Originally published in Australia, then in the UK, I bought the American rights to *Confessions of a Sociopathic Social Climber* by Adèle Lang for a small advance. (Don't worry—the author got royalties!) It was destined to be a small midlist book, and we ordered a print run of ten thousand copies. The publicist had sent the book out to all and sundry, including of course some long shots, and one of those came in. The editor of *Cosmopolitan* loved it. It was featured in their "Summer Beach Reads" section. Then, the *Cosmo* editor went on *Live! With Regis and Kelly* and told Kelly Ripa how much he loved the book! Kelly insisted on taking his copy right there, on the air, instead of waiting to get her own. And just when we thought it couldn't get any better, Kelly decided she wanted a "Reading with Ripa" book club (this was in the early 2000s, the heyday of TV book clubs). To make hers different, instead of looking for deep and serious books (read: depressing), she wanted to focus on summer beach reads. And *Confessions* was the second book selected! Four print runs later, we were officially on the *New York Times* list, and the author came over from England to tape an episode of *Live!* Later, *Confessions* was made into a TV movie starring Jennifer Love Hewitt and Joey Lawrence. This was an unknown author, with no U.S. platform, and the book would have normally had an unremarkable life, except for the enthusiastic publicist and some serious serendipity.

If this sounds like fun, by all means dive in! If it sounds exhausting, be wary and be forewarned. Publicists are under a lot of pressure to make every book into the success story I detailed above, but lightning doesn't strike every day. If you do want this job, be sure to emphasize your organizational skills as well as your social ones. Any kind of event planning is fantastic, but also be sure to include on your résumé any coordinating of large, complicated projects, dealing with difficult people, and networking. As with all jobs, keep the job description very much in mind when discussing your skills and talents.

Publicity assistants have the second-lowest starting salary after editorial assistants, as it is also a popular job. A publicity assistant will start out answering the phone and opening mail. They will coordinate a large number of mailings, track how publicity does—including keeping up with press clippings—and research media opportunities.

Chapter 8

Marketer

Marketing is a bit like publicity, but it's more low-key and creative and doesn't often deal with people outside of the publishing house.

Average starting salary in sales and marketing is $34,000, but sales skews that number higher. Marketing works very closely with sales.

This job needs an imaginative, thorough person who is good at seeing the big picture. Marketing usually splits into two components: marketing the publisher as an entity (to bookstores and other customers of the publisher) and marketing books to readers. Usually people in marketing stay in marketing. There's not as much burnout in this department. It's a fairly small department and as within the other departments, one starts out as an assistant.

Marketing works with the company website, including pages on Facebook, Twitter, Instagram, and Pinterest, and they put together the catalogs (which are mostly online) used by sales to sell the publisher's books. All the content on a publisher's website is the responsibility of marketing, from author interviews to blogs to news to events to ads. Most publishers also have multiple e-newsletters that marketing puts out.

Marketing (in conjunction with sales) decides which books should come with a display (called a "dump," they range in size from a small single-book countertop display to one-hundred-unit pallet displays), which books should have a reading group guide or a shelf talker, and which books would benefit most from being on the New Release table at Barnes & Noble. (You know publishers pay for that privilege, right?) They source, coordinate, and pay for any stickers, fixtures, and signs for store displays. They also work with social media on the consumer side, such as through Goodreads, as well as reaching out to fan clubs and special-interest groups. They create e-postcards, book trailers, and podcasts.

Marketing is the most technically savvy department these days. It is the one department where youth is more advantageous than experience. A bigger and bigger part of the job these days is working with book bloggers (although at some companies that's done by publicity), podcasters, and social media. They help set up Skype appointments for authors with book clubs and promote authors' book trailers.

This department usually also encompasses advertising, promotions, and co-op. Advertising and promotions are pretty self-explanatory. Co-op is more complicated. It's a fund of promotional money the publisher will pay to stores to "cooperatively" promote the publisher's titles. It works like this: Last year Bookstore A bought $X of books from Publisher M. That means this year Bookstore A's co-op budget is a percentage of X. They can use that money to pay for promotional costs, such as the cost of putting together the bookstore's newsletter, although they can only pay up to half of the costs with co-op (so if the newsletter costs a hundred dollars, they can get fifty dollars of co-op money back from publishers whose books they feature in the newsletter). One bookstore in Massachusetts even used their co-op money to pay for drinks after an author event. Each person at the event would get a ticket, and that ticket was redeemable for one drink at a bar a few storefronts up. It made for a very popular, memorable event!

Chapter 9

Sales Representative

S ales may be the most vital department of all. If the books don't sell, then everything else is fruitless. Even if you think you could never do sales, I'll bet you can sell books to book people.

This is one of the few jobs at the large publishers that allow you to live somewhere other than New York. The larger companies will usually have reps in the West Coast, the Mountains and Plains, the Midwest, New England, the Mid-Atlantic, and the Southeast, as well as international sales teams.

Sales reps earn on average $65,000 (not starting salary), as opposed to an average salary of $50,000 for editorial. It pays so well because the rest of the publishing industry generally looks down on sales. The sales reps are often considered the one noncreative role at the publishing house, and the creative types don't like how crass it can be to break down an author's life's work into simple dollars and cents, but publishing is a business. In addition to a salary, sales reps can earn a commission and substantial bonuses. A sales assistant can earn $31,000 to $44,000. A good rule of thumb: the less desirable a job is (in the book publishing world), the easier it is to get, the better it pays, and the better you are treated by your higher-ups. So don't dismiss sales out of hand just because you think you're not the sales type.

There are both national sales reps, dealing with companies like Barnes & Noble and Books-A-Million, and local sales reps who sell to independents. There are also reps who deal with wholesalers and with online retailers. Sales deals with nontraditional booksellers, like big-box stores, grocery stores, and specialty shops. Sales reps specialize in library and school accounts, as well as retail. Some sales reps work exclusively over the phone, speaking with accounts all day, helping with issues, taking orders, and explaining

A day in the life of a sales rep

My second job in sales was as the New England sales rep for a book wholesaler. I drove around New England visiting four or five bookstores a day. Hmm, doesn't sound so dreadful, does it? Unlike a wholesaler rep, a publisher rep will visit far fewer stores because their visits are longer. They sit down with the bookstore owner/manager/buyer, and the two of them page through the catalogs, discussing what is coming out next season from the publisher, and the bookstore tells the sales rep how many of each book the store will order. The sales rep uses the tip sheets (provided with the catalog) to tell the buyer what marketing is lined up, what publicity is in the works, if the book has gotten great prepublication reviews, if it's been sold widely abroad, if there's any tie-in to media, and what the author's platform is. Those tip sheets also include any comparable or competitive books, the author's previous publishing history, and any pertinent seasonal or timely information, such as a pitch for a book about chocolate as part of a Valentine's Day display or a note when Pet Adoption Month is.

As a wholesaler rep, my job was more about customer service and making sure stores knew about all the various services we offered, so I could do more strategic strikes and hit a larger number of stores in a day. I did once shovel my car out of two feet of snow in Maine while wearing heels and a skirt (in my defense, it was the end of April), and I now know what New Englanders mean by their jokes about mud season (aka spring). But I also got to go to Martha's Vineyard and Nantucket. Sure, not in season, but work paid! I finally got to fly first class, and I visited some very cool places. While, sadly, I wasn't able to stop at Ben & Jerry's, as they only give tours during the same hours that bookstore managers make appointments (between 10:00 and 5:00, so I didn't have to get up early!), I did get to go to some great places. My favorites were the museums, where I sometimes got personal and behind-the-scenes tours.

Obviously, my accounts weren't just bookstores—they were any independent store that sells books. I had a yarn store, a cookery store, a gardening store, and even a dog bakery on my list. They might have been a little unusual, but they did keep my days interesting! Being a road rep is really time-consuming, but it was fun for me.

new programs. If you like to travel, love bookstores, and are charming and a people person, this might be the right job for you.

A sales assistant is going to work with national account reps to coordinate multiple mailings to their buyers, make sure the buyers' orders are placed in a timely fashion and reflect the discussed amounts, run a variety of reports both for the reps and buyers, and expedite shipping of hot titles

from the publisher's warehouse or printers. Like all assistant positions, organization, scheduling, and attention to detail are the crucial traits to emphasize when applying for this job. There are fewer jobs in this area today with
the shrinking of bookstores over the last decade, but the attrition looks to
have stabilized, and just as many books are being sold now as before; it's just
the outlets that have shifted. There are more nontraditional accounts, from
Michael's to Home Depot to Sur La Table, and sometimes the sales department will sell to the stores directly, like with Urban Outfitters, or they will
work with a wholesaler who needs regular subject-specific lists for accounts,
like Whole Foods or Petco.

Chapter 10

Buyer

On the other side of the table from the publisher's sales rep is the bookstore's buyer, who determines which books will be featured prominently at their stores, which will have big displays, and which titles from a few months ago just aren't selling and need to be returned.

Buyers can be assigned to either a single publisher (or publisher group if dealing with small presses), to a genre, or to a `format`. The buyers need to find a balance between having enough stock to fill all orders and not having overstock. It's easy either to have tons of overstock and fill all orders, or to have low stock and fill very few orders. But a good buyer manages both.

The buyer's computer systems have a lot of data, especially on the store's backlist. It will tell you how many copies of a certain book the company sold during this week last year, in the last four weeks, the last four weeks averaged, year to date, last year, and so on. Some systems track demand as another data point, which can tell you if the sales might have been artificially low if stock ran out. That shows how many people tried—and failed—to order that book, which can indicate how much more over the average sales you should purchase, or else you'll just run right out again. It should also have information on seasonality, so you know to buy more of a Summer Reading book in the spring and more diet books in December, to be prepared. A lot of ordering is automated these days, but there are still exceptions that require a human eye. And the buying needs to be managed so you don't run out of money.

What do I mean by run out of money? Aren't you using someone else's money? Well, yes, you are, but there isn't an infinite amount of it just because it isn't yours. You often will be given an "open-to-buy," which is your budget.

One way to improve it is to process a return back to the publisher. Your same computer system, in addition to generating recommended buys, will also create recommended returns lists. These lists will show if you have a book selling on average ten copies a week, with four thousand books on hand, which means you have four hundred weeks' worth of books on hand. That's a problem. When I was a buyer, our goal was to have four weeks' supply on hand. We really wanted just one week, but with variable shipping times and reprint times, four weeks was much more reliable. If you're a buyer for a major chain bookstore, you want to have large quantities of New York Times best sellers on hand in all stores to make displays. But you want no more than a couple of copies of all other books, as you can get almost any book in one or two days from the wholesalers. Wholesalers want to have a broader selection of books in stock, as stores tend not to order best sellers from them, but instead order obscure titles. In fact, the sales of books by bestselling authors peak at wholesalers several books before they peak at retailers.

A junior buyer buys all the backlist, does backlist returns, maintains the title information in the systems, and preps for new-title (frontlist) buying sessions with the senior buyers. A junior buyer mostly keys orders over and over again for the same books.

There has to be something to keep you going, and that is new-title buying sessions! Seasonally you will get sets of catalogs from the publishers (mostly electronic these days.) You will first send them off to be entered into the system. When that is done, you have to go through each one and confirm they were set up correctly, as no one knows your publishers as well as you do, and often small (but important) details will be missed. Then you will do research on comparison/competitive titles. In addition to the catalogs, you also get tip sheets or sell sheets. These should each list a few comparison titles for every cataloged book. However, they usually list them only for the easy books and list nothing for the books with no obvious and simple comparisons. As junior buyer, you will come up with those on your own. If you are looking at a diet cookbook, you'll want to look up the sales of other diet cookbooks, preferably from the same publisher—none more than a few years old—in the same format, with a similar price point. And your senior buyer will look at how those other books have been selling and determine the new-title buy based mostly on the sales from those similar books. And they really need to be similar. You want to compare a British mystery to other British mysteries. You want to compare a New York–set chick-lit book to other New York–set chick-lit books. And the reason for using the same publisher is that some are better at particular genres than others. For instance, Tor is never going to be known for their literary fiction, and similarly W. W. Norton is never going to do a good job publishing romances. So you want to know if Sourcebooks is good at publishing cookbooks or if Wiley is good at business books. Otherwise you can end up over- or under-buying.

When I was a junior buyer, finding the comparison titles and the new-title buying sessions were definitely my favorite parts of the job. After that, my next favorite part was the relationships with the sales reps (and their assistants). Smart, bookish people, they were always fun to talk with. They would send copies of books (prepublication) that they thought we'd like, or we could request them. They did ask for a lot of reports, but those were easy to run. It was in their best interest to give us accurate information and not to try to force books down our throats. Media is unique in that all products (books, movies, music) are returnable, whereas most everything else in retail is not. So publishing sales reps saw a direct correlation to their bottom line if they suggested we buy a lot more of a book than we needed, as we would send them back. It's to their advantage to tell you if they think a book is a sleeper, if it's not an author's best work, if the early buzz is great or not great. That said, some buyers have a unique problem when publishers don't print enough of a hot title, and buyers have to negotiate to get as many books as possible to fill backorders. A buyer and a sales rep should have a cooperative relationship, not an adversarial one. Still, it's fun to be the buyer, as they are the one in the driver's seat in this relationship.

A junior buyer also is responsible for tracking hot shipments (for best sellers or books otherwise blowing up due to media), including working with warehouses to get the shipments expedited and to get them received, stocked, and stowed as soon as they arrive at the loading dock. You also need to cancel old purchase orders that were misreceived. The buyer selects books to be highlighted in marketing, either in a book promotion in the store or in a catalog or other materials (like the Pennie's Picks at Costco). The junior buyer coordinates with the marketing and sales reps to be sure that books being promoted are in stock in sufficient quantities. It's vital to keep abreast of publishing news and trends so you aren't caught off guard (and low on stock) when awards are announced, when major media hits, or when a TV or movie tie-in is released.

There's always something new. And the buyers know about all the about-to-be-published books first. It is a fun, challenging job. Yes, people are always threatening to replace buyers with computers, but that will never happen.

Readers' tastes are too fickle and unpredictable, and the book business doesn't do nearly enough research about what sells, what doesn't, and why. Without that information, buying systems will remain fancy calculators.

Salaries can vary widely, entirely depending on the store and the region. In addition to individual independent bookstores, this job can be found at chains, at non-bookstore chains that carry books (such as a pet store, grocery store, or hardware store), or book wholesalers. At chains and wholesalers, assistant buyer salaries start at around $30,000.

Chapter 11

Bookseller

The most useful experience you can have for a career in publishing is to work in a bookstore. Whether you want to work in editorial, design, sales, marketing, or any other department, you will learn so many invaluable lessons when working as a frontline bookseller that your future jobs will be made easier. This experience is valued in publishing, so it can help open doors.

Here are some tips that are relevant specifically to applying for a bookstore job (tips for applying for publishing jobs begin with chapter 17): Go during a weekday, when they aren't busy. Make eye contact. Dress business casual both for the application drop-off and the interview (I know most have online-only applications these days, but do this where possible). While dropping off the application (or after submitting an online one), ask to talk to a manager. Briefly chat with them, tell them how much you love to read, how you'd love to work in a bookstore, etc. Expect them in an interview to ask you the last five books you read. They expect to hear about current books, not Faulkner and Shakespeare, even if you are a student. They might ask you how you would recommend those books to a customer. They might ask you a question like, "If a customer came in and said they loved *The Help*, what else would you recommend to them?" (A hint: it's good to ask the customer what they liked about the book. You might recommend different books if they replied that they liked the women's relationship, the Southern setting, or the civil-rights story line.)

If the bookstore has only a café position open, take it, but keep reminding them that you want to switch to bookseller when a position opens up. The children's department isn't popular, so it might be easier to get a job if you're willing to work there (you should also know something about some children's books). Expect them to ask you to explain how any prior experience you may have will translate to the bookstore. Ideally, explain how you had an issue with a customer and worked it out to everyone's satisfaction. Expect a customer service–type question or two.

Also, ask around. I know networking can be confusing, but here's what I found out *after* I started working at the bookstore:

- Assistant manager Kay's best friend had worked with me at a previous job.

- Shipping & receiving supervisor Russell had been in my chemistry II class in high school.

- Bookseller Jim had been in my chemistry I class in high school.

- Supervisor Charles went to my college, and his little brother was in my class.

I got the job anyway, but it would have helped if I had been able to make any of those connections beforehand. You might not think you know anyone useful for networking, but it's just not true. What would happen if you posted on Facebook that you want to work in a bookstore and asked if anyone knows anyone who works in a bookstore anywhere. You might be surprised.

When you get the job and are helping actual customers, you'll hear them say things like "What an ugly cover" and "I'd never read a book by a woman" and "But that's a science fiction book. I'd never read that." While you may never be able to convince them to see things your way, you might learn A) what covers turn consumers off, B) that most women writing in typical male genres may want to consider obscuring their gender, or C) that while teen/ YA crossover books can break out, you can't otherwise count on buyers to see past the category.

I worked for three summers in customer service in a campus bookstore, and later for two years full-time in a chain store. There I was first a bookseller and then the shipping and receiving supervisor. In my years in a bookstore, I learned:

- Not all *New York Times* best sellers are bad. In fact, when I gave them a chance, I really liked a bunch of them, and maybe I shouldn't be such a literary snob.

- Oprah is a god. We all want her book club to come back.

- Books positioned `face out` sell.
- Spinner racks were invented as a torture device for booksellers.
- The books on the front tables are not what booksellers like, but are paid for by publishers.
- You can keep working when the power goes out, so long as you have a calculator and a pen.
- I will never again clean other people's bathrooms (yes, this was a job requirement four days each week).
- I am not cut out for retail. I learned I am not a people pleaser, and I work better in back-office scenarios.

There is a funny website called <u>Not Always Right</u> that tells horror stories of retail life, including at bookstores. My favorite was the woman who's looking for something that is "like a book, but not a book" (and no, it isn't a magazine).*

*It was a bookmark.

Chapter 12

Book Packager

A book packager puts a book together for a publishing house. Why are some books packaged? They may have a very marketing-heavy component, such as a TV-show tie-in; they may be very difficult and complicated to put together, with multiple authors and very design-heavy components, such as encyclopedias; or they may be licensed books with a lot of rights clearances, such as a book on major league baseball players. If a packager can present the finished product of a book that may be hard to put together or conceptualize, the publisher has a much easier job in selling it. They often have a lot of high-end photography specifically commissioned, and even technology, like in *Bird Songs: 250 North American Birds in Song* by Les Beletsky, which comes with a built-in digital audio player that plays two hundred fifty songs and calls.

These books can be religious, children's, photo books, crafts, or teen series and publish in many genres. Teen series are the most famous packaged books, such as the *Beacon Street Girls*, *The Clique* books, *Sweet Valley High*, and *Sisterhood of the Traveling Pants*, going all the way back to *Nancy Drew*. But other examples include *House Beautiful: Your Dream Bathroom*, *Our Sun: Biography of a Star*, *UMass Rising: The University of Massachusetts Amherst at 150*, and *Mom and Dad Are Palindromes*. A packaging company will come up with a book concept (often they sell the book at the concept stage so they're not taking a huge risk) and research and hire a writer (who normally is paid a flat fee and not a royalty). The packager will do the editing, layout, copyediting, proofreading, jacket design, and sell the finished product to a publishing house (or sometimes the publishing house has contracted with a packaging company to put a book together). Sometimes the publisher prints the book; sometimes the packager does. The publisher catalogs the book, sells it to the marketplace, and fulfills orders. The buyers of the book will have no idea that certain books in a publisher's catalog are packaged, as they appear the same as the books the publisher puts together themselves.

Packagers need most of the same people—editors, designers, copyeditors, marketers—as publishing houses. They're just companies you've likely not heard of. Some of the bigger packagers are Alloy Entertainment, becker&mayer!, Quirk Books, MTM Publishing, Amaranth Books, and Spooky Cheetah Press.

More resources:
BookEnds, LLC
American Book Producers Association
Seth Godin
How Publishing Really Works

Chapter 13

Publishing Lawyer

A few years ago I volunteered at a college preparedness nonprofit, and one Saturday a smart young girl at the center asked me about publishing jobs. She sheepishly admitted that she wasn't sure if she wanted to go into publishing or be a lawyer instead. "Instead?" I asked. "Why not both? You know, publishing has lawyers, too!" She was so happy! There's nothing a teenager likes more than not having to make a decision.

I took a class at NYU on publishing law and it was fascinating. Here is the current 2014 class description:

> Every publishing professional needs to understand the basics of publishing law in this litigious era. Editors must know when to flag content as potentially libelous, and all employees in media industries must have a knowledge of copyright, privacy, intellectual property, and other important legal issues. In this course, our faculty of experienced lawyers in the publishing industry presents the key concepts through real-world examples, case studies, and presentations from guest speakers. Students will explore legal issues in print and on the Web as blogging and sites like Facebook, Twitter, and YouTube create a wide range of new legal and ethical issues. The course will also provide an introduction to contracts and contract negotiation.

When I took the class nearly ten years ago, naturally there was no mention of blogging or Facebook or Twitter. But they still primarily fall under one of the two largest areas publishing lawyers deal with: copyright infringement. For instance, when a large excerpt from Sarah Palin's book was posted online by Gawker, the posters claimed it was legally fine due to "fair use." Fair use means you can use a small part of a written work—with credit—without permission. And it's for critical use only. So a reviewer can quote a few lines from a book. But it doesn't mean you can quote a large part, or quote it just to quote it, and not for critical reason. It can get tricky if, for instance, you're working on a book about a singer/songwriter and need to quote lyrics. They can't comprise "a significant portion," so the shorter the song, the shorter the allowable quote. Gawker lost and HarperCollins won, so you can deduce that their "fair use" theory wasn't too accurate.

The other most common type of law practiced at publishing houses is contract law. One fascinating part of my NYU class involved the instructor telling us about various celebrities who were unable to produce either a manuscript or an "acceptable" manuscript in a reasonable time frame. (Yes, all contracts have a delivery date, but most publishers aren't hard-nosed about it—unless they want to get out of the deal. I've seen them extended for several years fairly frequently.) Even celebrities with ghost writers are sometimes unable to produce a book that anyone will buy. Some commit pretty blatant copyright infringement by lifting large sections wholesale from other books. Naturally, the professor couldn't give us details about who these celebs were, but through a series of hints, we did figure out a couple that were amusing. When an author can't produce an acceptable manuscript, not only will the publisher not publish the book, but the author will need to repay any advances paid out so far.

Other potential legal issues that arise include libel, fraud (à la *A Million Little Pieces* by James Frey), and copyright and permission (quoting and using photos). Also, if a book is published about the FBI, CIA, or any other government organization, these organizations require their employees to sign contracts allowing the employer to vet the book and redact any parts they deem unsuitable for publication, presumably for national security issues.

As an editorial assistant, we would do legal reads on our travel books every fall before the new editions came out. We had to flag anything questionable for the lawyers to look at. For example, you can't say a neighborhood is safe, because if a traveler is attacked there, they can sue. You also can't say an establishment is "skanky" or "gross" for libel reasons, although you can say things that are provable and specific, such as it is unclean, or the rooms are small and unheated. You can't say it's okay to jump over a fence onto private property to go see a cool view. You can't advise people how to sneak illegal drugs into or out of a country. Basically, you need to be sure you're following local laws and also not opening up the publishing house to lawsuits. This was a pretty interesting task (plus it paid overtime!).

So you aspiring lawyers out there who also love books, don't despair! You can do everything you want to do. The legal departments of publishing houses are pretty decently paid, fairly quiet, and small—about six people even for the biggest houses. If they have a major lawsuit, they call in the law firm they have on retainer. And while it's a very under-the-radar area of the book business, it's safe to say that it's crucial.

Legal jobs at publishing houses are hard to come by because there are so few and turnover is low. Most intellectual property lawyers work at private law firms but specialize in copyright or libel. Lately there have been some very large lawsuits, one with Google regarding scanning books and free use, and an antitrust case with Amazon accusing all the big publishers (except Random House) of colluding. The main thing lawyers do in the publishing industry is protect authors from people using their content for free, just as this book you are reading is copyrighted and therefore protected from being copied and resold.

Part II

Types of Publishing Houses

Once you decide on a job or two (or three) that
you think would suit you well, where should you
work? Luckily, there are plenty of options.

Chapter 14

Big, Medium, Small

First, there are the major publishers, which are the ones you've probably heard of. There's Penguin Random House, Simon & Schuster, Harper-Collins, Hachette (formerly Time Warner), and Macmillan.

Those publishers are enormous and other publishers don't come close. The midsize publishers are quite a bit smaller, which include houses such as Houghton Mifflin Harcourt, Grove Atlantic, Scholastic, Norton, and Avalon.

Then there are thousands of small publishers, some of which are very literary, such as Four Walls Eight Windows and Graywolf Press; others that are regional, such as John F. Blair in North Carolina and Hangover Productions in New York; and others that specialize in a single type of book, such as Health Communications Inc., Rodale Books, or MERCK Publishing.

Now, you might be thinking, wait a minute, I know there are a lot more big publishers than what she just listed. What about Knopf, Ballantine, Plume, Putnam, Dutton, and Berkley? Well, those are all imprints. Knopf and Ballantine are two of the seventy-four imprints or divisions of Random House; Plume, Putnam, Dutton, and Berkley are all parts of Penguin. Those publishers recently merged to form the biggest publisher ever. I worked at Thomas Dunne Books, which is an imprint of St. Martin's Press, which is a division of Macmillan. If you really want to specialize in a type of genre, like mysteries, or science fiction, or travel, then you ought to apply directly to those imprints.

Remember, size is relative. For this list I'm considering publishers from the point of view of their American trade publishing (or general-interest) divisions only. If you take into account all divisions, such as international and textbooks, John Wiley is 50 percent bigger than Simon & Schuster, and

McGraw-Hill is more than twice the size of HarperCollins. Oxford University Press is bigger than Harlequin, which is bigger than Marvel Comics, but those numbers don't reflect how those publishers are perceived in the trade marketplace.

There are advantages and disadvantages working at large, medium-size, and small publishers. Large publishers have more money, can publish more books, have more opportunities for advancement, and always have a lot of excitement going on. However, some large houses are very corporate, some make it extremely hard to advance, and it's hard to stand out in a large pool of employees. The smaller the house, the more opportunities you have to shine, and the more risk there is to crash. You get a better chance to see how all the departments work, and at some houses you might actually *be* three or four departments. But with smaller houses come smaller budgets for publicity and author advances, thus increasing the difficulty of competing with publishing conglomerates. Many agents will take an equal offer from a larger publishing house for the security of the large sales force, well-connected publicity department, and prestige. But smaller houses can publish more unusual, riskier books. Smaller houses are also everywhere, so if you want to live in Texas, Minnesota, or Washington, you still have options.

In a February 2014 interview with *Guernica*, Elisabeth Schmitz, the editorial director of Grove Atlantic said:

What about self-publishing?

You've probably heard a lot about self-publishing in the last few years, and you might even be getting some pushback from family and friends that you shouldn't go into book publishing because it'll soon be an extinct industry due to self-publishing. First of all, the death knell of publishing has been rung dozens of times, without panning out. I love the January 9, 2010, Fresh Eyes column summarizing publishing forecasts from *Harper's* magazine, dating back to 1850. Within my lifetime I remember hearing that print book publishing was soon to die due to the advent of books on tape and later CD-ROMs. Neither happened. Yes, there will continue to be changes, same as ever. The trade paperback and the mass market paperback both created major changes in publishing, but neither vanquished the hardcover.

Instead of looking at self-publishing as a reason not to get into publishing, view it as an opportunity. There are dozens of companies that help authors with their publications, from simple uploading of the manuscript, to editing help, to cover design, to marketing and publicity, and so on. Some of the larger players in this field currently are: CreateSpace (Amazon), Author Solutions (owned by Penguin), Smashwords, Lulu, BookBaby, INscribe Digital, and NOOK Press (B&N). And then there are businesses like Constellation, Perseus's digital distribution service for independent publishers to exploit the sales and marketing opportunities created by digital technology, and Lightning Source (Ingram), where authors can utilize their POD technology. These businesses are very technology-heavy, so they have great jobs for the IT-inclined.

While the quality of self-published books might not always be up to snuff, you would be helping authors fulfill their dreams. And there are, of course, books that started out as self-published and were so successful, they were picked up by traditional publishers, such as *The Joy of Cooking* by Irma Rombauer and *The Elements of Style* by William Strunk and E. B. White, and more recently *The Lace Reader* by Brunonia Barry and *Still Alice* by Lisa Genova.

"I think, contrary to some of the gloomy predictions for the book world, it's a good time to be a medium-size independent publisher like us. Some of the corporate publishers are forced to be commercial and sometimes ruthless about things, and they lose some great books and authors because of it. These are authors who we can then pick up and present to audiences in a different way. There's a real place for places like us and Norton, McSweeney's, Milkweed, and Graywolf now. There are readers who want to buy these books."

Chapter 15

Adult vs. Children's

Children's publishing has all of the same jobs and requirements as adult publishing, but children's and adult publishing are very separate, so you'll need to decide early on in your career which you'd rather do. Children's has many more opportunities for subrights sales, and those ancillary products need to be monitored to ensure they stay on message. Children's book editors work with schools and teachers and may produce teachers' guides or giant books. They are much more media-friendly. They work with both media products (*Teen Beach Movie, Dora the Explorer*) and market their products using media (Library Thing, podcasts, Twitter). Children's presents a lot more opportunities for tie-ins, events, and creativity. There are also more complications: from working with illustrators to dealing with reading levels and book bannings. Children's books are a pretty stable market for a variety of reasons. Books are a popular gift for children. Parents and grandparents— even those who don't read—will buy books for children. Backlist titles tend to stick around for decades as parents and grandparents buy books they themselves loved as children, for the child in their lives.

Children's books have a much wider range of genres and formats, mostly based around age and reading ability. For infants, cloth books, `board books` (with very hard cardboard pages that can stand up to chewing), and bath books (which are plastic and can get wet) are the first books, followed by picture books. Picture books can be long or short and can have no words or a thousand words, so they can be appropriate for children from zero to eight. When children start reading chapter books, many early reader books are further subclassified into stages. Toward the end of elementary school most children graduate to middle grade books, and in junior high they move on to

A career in children's books

by Sarah Dotts Barley, Editor, HarperCollins Children's Books

I've noticed a few common traits among children's book professionals. A few worth mentioning are:

A strong attendance record at the local independent bookstore or library's story time between the ages of birth to eight

A love of very long books and series that seem to never end (*Redwall*, *Harry Potter*, *Little House*)

A secret wish to have been sent off to boarding school at a very young age

A love of reading across genres

Of course, people come to publishing and children's book publishing from all sorts of backgrounds. I even know fellow editors who didn't love reading until they were much older and want to make sure that there are books out there for reluctant young readers! But, for the most part, I think that most of us chose children's and young adult publishing because that's the age we were when we all fell in love with reading and stories. When we read children's and YA books, we became lifelong readers.

There are also a few distinct differences I've seen between the children's book and the general or "grown-up" book worlds. A few of them are:

At any children's publisher, there is likely going to be a focus on the backlist. The industry is changing quickly, and in just the past seven years, I've watched children's publishing start to follow a more publishing event–driven model that took hold long ago in the adult book world. That said, the classics are alive and well in the children's book world, because so much of our business is driven by backlist. Parents and teachers want to buy books for their students and children that have already stood the test of time. A solid, healthy backlist enables us to take chances on new authors and types of books—hopefully authors and books that will one day help build the house's backlist for the artists who will take risks in the future.

The gatekeepers can truly make books for us. Teachers, librarians, reviewers—these smart people have a huge amount of influence on what books catch on in the market. A book can be beloved in-house, but books that really take off usually have huge champions in the school or library world. A great recent example of this was the groundswell of support across the country for Katherine Applegate's middle-grade novel *The One and Only Ivan*, which went on to win the hearts of children, parents, and the American Library Association's Newbery committee. Publishers' relationships and access to the gatekeepers in schools and libraries are critical in finding a wonderful book its readers.

All departments, but especially production, editorial, and design, work together to produce our final books. Our art director or designer will work on every aspect of the book—from the interior design to the jacket art. Ideally, the paper, the fonts, and all elements of the package work together to create one beautiful object that's worthy of becoming a part of a child's—or teen's—forever library.

One thing that drew me in particular to editing children's books was the sheer diversity of books published. And at every place I've worked, an editor can work on all kinds of books, so long as they are well written, tell a good story, and contribute in some way to the publisher's larger publishing mission. In any given day, I could work on a picture book about the environment, a voice-driven YA manuscript with a runaway narrator's point of view, or a funny history of the Bill of Rights. (Actually, I worked on all three of those things last Friday!) I like to read all kinds of books. Mysteries, sad books, funny books, historical fiction, contemporary fiction, romance, fantasy, realistic—it's fun to read and work on different kinds of things. It's never boring.

Lastly, children's book people are usually in a good mood.

In closing, I leave you with the legendary children's book editor Ursula Nordstrom's take on career opportunities in book publishing:

"Did I ever tell you ... I was taken out to luncheon and offered, with great ceremony, the opportunity to be an editor in the adult department? ... I almost pushed the luncheon table into the lap of the pompous gentleman opposite me and then explained kindly that publishing children's books was what I did, that I couldn't possibly be interested in books for dead dull finished adults, and thank you very much but I had to get back to my desk to publish some more good books for bad children." (from *Dear Genius: The Letters of Ursula Nordstrom*, collected and edited by Leonard S. Marcus, Harper, 1998)

young adult or (YA). After that is a new genre, new adult, which covers the college years or very early twenties. Series are big in children's books, and because of demand from schools, biographies and other nonfiction are also widely produced, although they don't get the publicity of fiction. The most notable awards in this category are the Caldecott Medal for illustrations (therefore, this normally goes to a picture book) and the Newbery Medal for story (normally given to a middle grade or YA chapter book).

Children's books, at least the illustrated ones, do not translate to e-books as well as adult books do. Since the font and formatting of e-books are adjustable, the illustrations and images can end up far away from the text they're supposed to illustrate. Also, many children's books are interactive, with pop-ups and pull tabs and stickers and other treatments that don't translate to e-books well. A few children's books have been successfully translated into apps, but as those need to be done one at a time, the market for children's e-books is growing slowly. Similarly, bookstores that focus on children's books have been more resilient to both showrooming and the economic decline. (Parents and grandparents are likely to cut their own personal book spending before spending on their children and grandchildren.)

Chapter 16

Other Publishers

Other possibilities for jobs are university presses, scholarly and reference, educational publishing, religious publishing, audio publishers, large-print publishers, and Book of the Month Club. With changes in technology, jobs in educational publishing are changing dramatically, and it's the division in the industry undergoing the most upheavals—keep that in mind before applying for jobs in that field. On the other hand, there are a lot of openings in digital publishing and even at self-publishing companies.

Digital publishing is an up-and-coming section. Traditional publishing houses are trying to digitize their backlist, but the biggest hurdle there is the contracts. Most contracts pre-2000 did not account for digital rights one way or the other. Publishers are claiming the digital rights are included among the variety of formats. Authors and agents say they aren't listed, so they aren't included and have to be negotiated for separately. When the legal issues are resolved, then the problem is actually converting the text to digital. Most pre-2000 books were printed off film, and not off digital files, so either the whole book needs to be digitally shot, or if there isn't a clean enough copy for that or if technical issues prevent it, it has to be reconstructed from scratch.

There are also self-publishing companies and divisions, such as Author-House (owned by Penguin), Create Space (Amazon), Publish America, Lulu, Smashwords, and IngramSpark. These companies help authors who have decided to forego the traditional publishing route and instead do it themselves. Self-publishing companies have editors, copyeditors, marketing, and publicists too, but their jobs are slightly different. As they're not acquiring books for a publishing house, but instead working on whatever comes in and whatever the authors pay for, there's not much back-and-forth, and there don't need to be meetings to discuss titles and book covers and marketing plans. As the publishers have no money on the line, they also have no say in those decisions, which are entirely up to the author. It should mean less pressure—after all, without the publisher making any decisions, the book's sales don't reflect back on the staff who worked on it. The quality of books generally isn't as high, and the manuscripts may be frustrating to work on, especially as there is not the buffer of an agent when dealing with authors.

University presses and PTR (Professional, Textbooks, and Reference) are good places to look for a job, as there isn't as much competition. The books and projects can be much drier, as most of the books are very technical and not much fun, but the profit margins can be better, as getting a textbook picked up by a college guarantees a certain number of sales, and knowing you are influencing a generation of students can be a heady experience. As mentioned earlier, the production of these books can be very complicated, with charts, graphs, sidebars, quizzes, and so on. The copyediting and proof-reading is even more crucial, and indexing is lucrative (if a pain in the neck). E-books in the textbook world have been slower to catch on than people expected, but the curve is headed upward. Working with grade schools and colleges can be inspiring, and you know you are helping kids learn.

Religious publishing is not just about Bibles. It encompasses every genre that trade publishing does, but almost always with a spiritual angle, including novels and books on politics, relationships, and even cooking. Not just trea-tises for churches, religious books fall into every area of life and are marketed in very mainstream stores, like Kmart and Books-A-Million.

Audio publishing is growing as commutes are lengthening, and with the increasing popularity of iPods and iPhones, programs like Audible and audiobooks.com are booming. Making an audiobook can be a tricky process. Just the right narrator has to be found and hired, studio time booked, and it's important that foreign-language words, colloquial phrases, and proper names are all pronounced correctly. Abridgements used to be the standard, but listeners are leaning much more toward unabridged recordings these days, even if some of them may be upward of thirty hours long. If you're taking a cross-country road trip, training for a marathon, or just don't like to garden in silence, audio books can be a perfect way to squeeze even more books into a hectic schedule. They can also help reluctant readers who may have learning or reading disabilities, such as dyslexia.

Part III

How to Get Into Publishing

After you've decided what type of job you think
you'd be good at doing and where you think
you'd most like to work, the question then
becomes: How do I get a job?

Chapter 17

Preparing for the Job Search

Research

Publisher and agency websites are the best places to start. Some smaller literary agencies, particularly ones that handle a couple of very big-name authors and aren't looking to acquire new client authors, do not have a website but that isn't necessarily a sign that something is wrong. They just have enough revenue not to need to worry about marketing or promoting themselves.

You'll want to work at a publisher or agency whose books you generally like, so browse in a bookstore, check out your shelves at home, surf online bookstores, join Goodreads or a similar site, and keep notes. Then look up those publishing houses or agencies. Check out their websites; see who else they publish or represent.

If you are a college student, many colleges participate in programs like BARC (the Big Apple Recruiting Consortium) or SLAC (Selective Liberal Arts Consortium) that organize trips to New York over spring break for interviews in the media industry, including publishing.

If you're serious about getting a job, you must be on LinkedIn. How is your LinkedIn profile looking? Have you been connecting with people? Look for people who went to your college who work in publishing and introduce yourself. You need to ask for recommendations from people you've worked with. Join your alumni group and publishing groups.

Subscribe to or bookmark Ask a Manager. When you are procrastinating, go there and read old posts. People write in and ask her questions—sometimes ridiculous ones. She is hilarious and has great advice. It's not just about job hunting; it's also about job having and job keeping and some of it won't be very pertinent (yet!), such as advice to managers about dealing with difficult employees, but the blogger does have a ton of great advice about résumés, interviews, references, and so on. And the other info will be useful eventually, so sock it away for the future.

Listen to episode #78 of the Books on the Nightstand podcast, which talks about getting a job in publishing. This podcast is two Random House sales reps talking about all things related to books, so it's a great resource for a variety of reasons.

So you still want to be an editor? Tips for job hunting:

If I haven't dissuaded you from pursuing editorial, here are job-hunting tips for how to go about looking for and getting an editorial job. Nearly all of this information applies to hopeful literary agents as well.

Sign up for Publishers Marketplace's free daily e-newsletter, Publishers Lunch, which has updates on publishing industry news. For instance, if you hear about a new imprint starting up at a house, then you'll know to apply there right away. And if someone left Publishing House A as an associate editor in order to become an editor at Publishing House B, then probably Publishing House A has an opening for an editorial assistant to replace him. Also they send out a weekly roundup of the deals made, which is another way to see what agents and editors like which sorts of books. Subscribe to Shelf Awareness and Publishers Weekly Daily (you do need a subscription to the print *Publishers Weekly* to sign up for the e-newsletter). Mediabistro also has publishing job listings.

In addition to standard web searches, you might check out the reference book LMP, Literary Market Place, which most libraries carry. The LMP is on the web, but you need a password (it's expensive). They list every legitimate publisher and agency. Writer's Digest's annual *Writers Market* book also has an exhaustive list of agencies and publishers and will describe what types of books they're currently acquiring.

First, you should find which editors' and agents' books you'd most enjoy working on. You can often find the name of the editor and agent on the acknowledgments page or through Google. In addition to figuring out what kinds of books you like and would like to work on, also think about what books you hate. That, I find, is actually more telling than what you like. For example, I found *The Bridges of Madison County* very manipulative, and to me it felt like an exercise in marketing. I thought *Cloud Atlas* was pretentious and gimmicky. And *The God of Small Things* to me read like a college creative writing class assignment: full of navel-gazing, with a ridiculous ending contrived solely for shock value. The common thread through these books is that I highly value honesty and authenticity, and I do not appreciate books trying to be more than they are. Your literary pet peeve may be magical realism or unreliable narrators or unlikable main characters.

Spend an hour at your local bookstore and really look at every section. You should pick several categories. Include categories other than literary fiction and narrative nonfiction because those are what *everyone* new to publishing says they want to work in. Not only do those books normally not sell well, but you want to stand out from the crowd. Some sections, like Reference and cooking and travel, are going away because of the internet, so those wouldn't be good subcategories to specialize in. This is a business, not a charity, and publishers want to make money.

What makes money? Again, do your homework. Find at least one category that regularly performs well that you can stomach and be sure to mention that one. Although I really wanted to acquire literary fiction and narrative nonfiction (and I sometimes did), the books I acquired that were big financial successes were chick-lit, pop culture, and humor.

Think about the personal finance category, for instance. Maybe due to your parents' careers you have spent a lot of time around finance and can help explain it to laypeople. Do you like how-to books or science books for regular people? If you had all the time and money in the world, what books (other than literary fiction and narrative nonfiction) would fill your bookshelves? By the way, if you still want to put narrative nonfiction on your list, you need to be more specific. Employers want to know if you like travel memoirs or food memoirs or finding one's self memoirs or addiction memoirs or fish out of water memoirs. And for fiction, you also should be more specific. Do you like Southern fiction (and if so, what variety—cutesy and quaint? Quirky and odd? Dark and melodramatic?), mysteries (hard-boiled? Cozy? In translation Scandinavian? Series?), romances (regency? Contemporary? Historical? With vampires, pirates, or cowboys?), and so on. You need to be able to drill down to the exact things in each genre that you like and why. Be wary of jumping on currently popular bandwagons, as those often have already peaked, and editors are looking for the next big thing, not the last big thing.

As an example, I like chick-lit—*but* not those about the twenty-two-year-old with four roommates who hates her job and just happens to have a super cute, funny, nice male friend who she doesn't like in *that* way. And really, I'm so tired of her working in publishing or magazines and living in New

York or London, I'm going to throw it across the room. I prefer chick-lit like Jennifer Weiner's *Good in Bed*—a late-twenties woman with a real job and real problems (accidental pregnancy, premature birth, baby with serious medical/health problems) who lives in Philadelphia and is a little fat. It's a fine line, I know, but as soon as an agent sent me a chick-lit novel with the woman living in Atlanta, working as a wedding coordinator (who likes her job), with a great boyfriend who proposes, but to whom she says no and doesn't quite know why, I jumped on it and bought it. That was an agent who paid attention! (The book is called *Toss the Bride*.)

You certainly don't have to know exactly what you like down to the level that I just explained, but it's good to know if you like biographies of politicians, historical figures, celebrities, or ordinary people doing extraordinary things. Being able to speak to this type of specificity regarding genre will impress an editor or agent and indicate your thoughtfulness about and full knowledge of the industry.

Many adults who haven't read children's books in many years dismiss picture books as cloyingly sweet treacle that would rot their teeth (and soul) and that they would hate working on. While a few of those do exist, you don't have to acquire those kinds of picture books. If you look into the genre further, you will find hilarious and even subversive books like *Scaredy Squirrel, I Must Have Bobo!, Born Yesterday, Shark vs. Train, Jeremy Draws a Monster*, and *I Want My Hat Back*. The best picture books are funny and also speak wryly to parents in a way that kids don't pick up on.

Be sure to read job descriptions to help tailor your résumé and cover letter to point out that you do have the specific skills requested. Think carefully about what skills and personality traits are right for the job you want and therefore ought to be emphasized. You may be surprised by how you can spin your experiences to work for you. For instance, after college I worked as a bartender. At that job, I learned how to be extremely diplomatic, not easily insulted, and work in high-pressured situations. A cover letter is the perfect place to explain what transferable experiences you gained from a seemingly unrelated job. If you have any experience with clerical work, remember that it is the bulk of the job description of an editorial assistant. If you have a degree in a liberal arts field, they already assume you can write, so that's not necessary to mention. Do not tell them you're an aspiring author, as that doesn't impress them, and makes them think you're not serious about wanting to be an editor or agent, but instead are simply marking time until you can impose on your colleagues.

Know what you've read to be ready for the interview

Keep a list of the books that you read. Join a website like Goodreads, LibraryThing, Shelfari, weRead, TheReadingRoom, Libib, Booklamp, Reader2, aNobii, Riffle, BookLikes, ThirdScribe, or Slice Bookshelf. Or buy a book log—really any ordinary notebook will do. You might think you'll be able to remember all the books you read, but as the years pile on and more and more books end up on your "read" list, it will become harder to remember all of them. If you have a particularly bad memory, like I do, short reviews will also come in handy later when you're looking at a book you're certain you read (you may even know the exact date thanks to your records!) but can't for the life of you remember anything about it.

These lists will be useful later. Editors and agents need to brainstorm comparison titles, checking that another book just like this one hasn't already been published. Or it's good to have this list to consult as you decide what genres to specialize in, and when you're trying to distill your personal likes and dislikes to explain to agents

You'll notice I've not yet mentioned contacting human resources. In my experience that route has been less than helpful the majority of the time. Applying through them certainly can't hurt, and I'm sure some HR departments are excellent, but I have found that to be the case only once in my career. If possible, going the direct route is usually the most efficient and best option—straight to the person who will be doing the hiring and will be your boss.

Preparing for the Interview

You don't want to be Maxwell Perkins, Ernest Hemingway and F. Scott Fitzgerald's editor. He is dead. Keep in mind you are looking for a job in this century. Many wannabe editors say they want to discover the next Hemingway, the next Faulkner, the next Wolfe. Really? The next drunk, misogynist ass who also happens to be dead? And whose books would have been out of print eighty years ago if it weren't for required summer reading? This does not impress an interviewer.

It's great if you've read the classics. Many would argue it's essential to know the background for how we got to today (although any humanities degree that involves a lot of reading is just fine for a career in publishing—political science, history, philosophy, etc.). But do try to remember what century we're living in. You will be asked what books you've read recently. And they should be recently published books. In fact, if you have time before your interview, you should run out and buy some books published by the actual publishing house (and division or imprint) where you are interviewing. Drop everything and read. It might be difficult, but you should be able to read a short book a day if you otherwise do nothing else, and so you should be able to get through three or four before your interview. Even if you're in town and free immediately, it's best to ask for an interview a couple of days out, to give yourself time to prep.

Catch up on the *New York Times* best sellers. If that previous sentence made you throw up in your mouth a little bit, you may want to reconsider your prospective career, or at least make an adjustment so you're applying only to university presses. They're very important. If you want a job at Random House or HarperCollins, they want best sellers. You don't have to read a bunch of trash in preparation; you can pick and choose. There are twenty-one *New York Times* lists to choose from, and most of the lists have up to thirty-five titles. There are other best seller lists you can choose among as well. If you want more literary choices, your best bet is the IndieBound lists.

When choosing what books to catch up on, most English majors haven't read much nonfiction. Nonfiction is easier to promote, which means it's easier to sell, which means it's easier to buy as an editor. (When booking authors for interviews, it's so much easier to come up with questions for a nonfiction author than for a novelist. There are more angles, more

what you're looking for. It's not necessary to be a speed reader in this business, but it sure can help as a great deal of reading is inevitable (and the more you read, the faster you will get, so don't despair, slow readers!). You can even keep lists of things like book covers you love and books you want to buy.

How to choose what to read

When you've pretty much been reading only books assigned in school for most of your life, looking through the fiction department or even the new releases at your local bookstore can be daunting. How do you pick from all the hundreds and thousands of choices? How do you pick books that are good, that are well written, that you'll enjoy, and that people in publishing are reading?

The easiest step is to talk to a bookseller. Hopefully you have read and liked one or two nonschool books that you can offer up, so the bookseller can suggest others with a similar feel and tone. Most bookstores have a "staff recommends" shelf, which is invariably a good source (libraries often have this too).

Goodreads recommends books to you based on books you shelve, so the more you list, the better the recommendations will be. You can also friend others on the site and see what they're reading, and check out different lists of books. Subscribe to BookPage's e-newsletters, including their "book of the day." Also subscribe to the "For Readers" e-newsletter of Shelf Awareness. Both of these resources are excellent, and they curate their reviews (they don't review just anything). They are grouped into genres that are useful and geared toward readers rather than industry professionals. Book blogs and book podcasts are also great resources.

Publishers Marketplace compiles all of the book industry best-of lists for each year. Click on the tab for Industry Lists, and then Publishers Lunch Best of the Best. If you are price-sensitive and prefer paperbacks, don't look at this year's as those will all be hardcovers. Look at the last two years' and you should find some excellent recommendations. And they are in ranked order, so for instance the first book in 2012 fiction, *Bring Up the Bodies*, was on ten different lists and won one major prize.

If you are dead-set on the classics and can't wrap your mind around anything else, pick up books like *Havisham* by Ronald Frame, *Longbourn* by Jo Baker, or *Mrs. Poe* by Lynn Cullen. These are all new novels based on books or authors considered classics (*Great Expectations, Pride and Prejudice*, and Edgar Allan Poe respectively).

If you want to explore nonfiction but are stumped, the key phrase to look for is a book that "reads like a novel"; check out memoirs, which feel very much like novels. Start with history, which is very story-driven, and from there branch out into subject areas that interest you. Whether you love music or running or cooking, there are great books on every topic.

talking points, more easily targeted readers. For example, with a health book you can go to whatever organization targets that issue, like the American Heart Association or the Juvenile Diabetes Research Foundation, and get their help in promoting the book. Historical societies are always interested in histories, and with a political book you have a shot at getting on *The Daily Show*. Novels, however, unless they have a health, history, or political angle, can be very hard to get attention for. Narrative nonfiction reads too much like fiction and tends to have fewer hooks, so it gets lumped in the same pile with fiction when it comes to publicity and sales.)

After you're asked what books you've read recently, you may be asked which book you liked most and why, or you may be asked more specific questions about a particular title: if you liked it or not, what you thought, if you would have done anything differently in the publication of the book. If you intend to try to bullshit your way through this question, be careful. I wouldn't spout off a string of books you haven't read. Don't worry about saying you dislike a book if you did. It shows you are discerning, have a critical eye (key for an editor), and are willing to give your opinion despite it potentially being in the minority (naturally if any book is a best seller, disliking it will be a minority viewpoint).

Additionally, you will be expected to be familiar with the publisher and imprint where you are interviewing. If you go to Minotaur (a mystery imprint) and ramble on about horror books, or to NAL (a romance and Western imprint) and talk about literary fiction, or to Knopf (a literary imprint) and talk about your love of romances, you've not done your home-work. Some of the more mainstream divisions will be harder to pigeonhole than the genre ones, so with those you'll want to spend more time memo-rizing the lists, looking up the books, and reading descriptions.

Just as I imagine doctors are annoyed watching *E.R.* and lawyers are annoyed by *The Good Wife*, I read (and watch) these interpretations of publishing with trepidation. I do not watch *Castle*, although fifteen years ago I did watch *Stark Raving Mad*, the very short-lived TV show where Neil Patrick Harris played the editor to Tony Shalhoub's quirky, reclusive, best-selling novelist. *The Proposal* is pretty accurate, though the publishing story drops out of it pretty early on. By far the best publishing movie is *The Last Days of Disco*, set in the early eighties. It name-drops real-life publishers, and when there's an editorial problem, the solution is both brilliant and very ahead of its time. (And apparently, this movie was later published as a novel, which is now out of print.) I will also admit that I really liked the TV show

Stacked, starring Pamela Anderson, although that was about a bookstore, not publishing, but I have already said I think everyone who works in publishing should do a stint in a bookstore. (Funny trivia: *Stacked* was on Fox, which is owned by Rupert Murdoch, who also owns HarperCollins. So the set for the bookstore was completely filled with Harper books and promotional pieces. They were almost all damaged and defective books. So many more of them were `spine out` on the shelves than is normally done on a TV show fake bookstore, but conveniently that made it more accurate for how a real bookstore is.) But I am not a big fan of *You've Got Mail*, where the put-upon independent bookstore owner buys her coffee at Starbucks (not at an independent coffee shop) and randomly picks up stacks of books and puts them down elsewhere in the store for no reason.

The Devil Wears Prada takes place in magazine publishing, not book publishing, but the two industries are first cousins. It hit a little close to home as some bosses *are* that bad. While all industries have bad bosses, an industry that rewards people by letting them name a division after themselves and put their name on all the books does tend to create oversize egos at a higher rate.

Youngblood Hawke by Herman Wouk and *No Angel* by Penny Vincenzi are fun historical novels about the industry. Not very useful, but entertaining nonetheless.

Additional reading

Fiction:
  Blind Submission by Debra Ginsberg
  How I Became a Famous Novelist by Steve Hely
  The Novel by James A. Michener

Books about editors:
  Max Perkins: Editor of Genius by A. Scott Berg
  Another Life: A Memoir of Other People by Michael Korda
  Dear Genius: The Letters of Ursula Nordstrom collected and edited by Leonard S. Marcus

Books about publishing houses:
  Hothouse: The Art of Survival and the Survival of Art at America's Most Celebrated Publishing House, Farrar, Straus and Giroux by Boris Kachka
  Golden Legacy: How Golden Books Won Children's Hearts, Changed

Publishing Forever, and Became an American Icon Along the Way by Leonard S. Marcus

Books about books:

How a Book Is Made by Aliki

Margaret Mitchell's Gone With the Wind: A Bestseller's Odyssey from Atlanta to Hollywood by Ellen F. Brown and John Wiley Jr.

Girl Sleuth: Nancy Drew and the Women Who Created Her by Melanie Rehak

The Professor and the Madman: A Tale of Murder, Insanity, and the Making of the Oxford English Dictionary by Simon Winchester

Other books about the book world:

The King's English: Adventures of an Independent Bookseller by Betsy Burton

Book Business: Publishing Past, Present, and Future by Jason Epstein

Book One: Work, 1986–2006 by Chip Kidd

Lord of Publishing: A Memoir by Sterling Lord

The Subversive Copy Editor: Advice from Chicago by Carol Fisher Saller

The Everything Store: Jeff Bezos and the Age of Amazon by Brad Stone

An Alphabetical Life: Living It Up in the World of Books by Wendy Werris

Chapter 18

Job Listings

There are a lot of websites you can use to look for publishing jobs. *Publishersweekly.com, publishersmarketplace.com, mediabistro.com,* and *bookjobs.com* will be the most helpful. The large and midsize publishers have job postings on their websites. Be sure to read job descriptions to help tailor your résumé to point out you do have those specifically requested skills. Think carefully about what skills and personality traits are right for the job you want and, therefore, ought to be emphasized in interviews and on résumés. You may be surprised how you can spin your experiences to work for you.

Keep in mind, better-paying jobs are often the less popular ones. Therefore, production and sales pay more, as do publishing houses with unpleasant work environments. So if you see a higher-than-usual salary posted, ask around. You may find out that the publishing house in question never promotes anyone, won't allow editorial assistants to meet with agents (and considers it a fireable offense if you do), or has a particularly awful boss at the helm of the department.

Larger companies use software programs to analyze the majority of job applications. To make it past this first hurdle, you need to use many of the exact keywords from the job listing in your résumé and cover letter.

Lost in translation: what job postings really say

Here's a look at some actual entry-level job listings. I have analyzed what they are really saying, and what a job seeker should see and respond to in these posts. I have removed the identifying information about the company.

JOB LISTING 1

Subsidiary Rights Assistant.
Candidate should have experience in book publishing, preferably in subsidiary rights. *Wow, that's really specific. While having prior experience is great, experience in subrights is unlikely for an entry-level position. Also note it says "should" not "must." Lacking experience is not a good excuse not to apply.* Candidate must also be extremely organized and have a demonstrated ability to handle a large workflow. *There will be a ton of paperwork and scheduling, and you'll probably be putting in more than forty hours a weeks.*

This position will support the Subsidiary Rights Department, reporting to the Director of Subsidiary Rights. *That is likely who you'll be interviewing with, so now you can Google them to find out A) whom to apply to (never apply only through HR), B) whom to address your cover letter to, and C) everything you can about them so you won't be surprised in your interview.*

Primary Responsibilities:

- Process and track foreign/domestic contracts, tax forms, and payments.

- Organize mailings and submissions for foreign/domestic subagents and publishers.

- Organize and prepare rights guides and arrangements for international book fairs.

- Provide administrative support for the Subsidiary Rights Department.

Your résumé and cover letter must emphasize your organizational skills. If you've worked as an assistant in an office, detail that. If you've organized an event for your fraternity, or a volunteer group, a reception, or really anything at all, be sure to talk it up. This is not only a very important part of the job, but the fact that they've now mentioned it four times indicates that odds are good the last person wasn't very well organized and you might be coming into a mess.

Required Skills: *Remember, even though they say required, these are more likely their "wish list."*

- Ability to prioritize, meet deadlines, and work independently. *This means your boss won't be around much. It's good to mention if you're a self-starter.*

- Exceptional organizational and interpersonal skills. *Wow, this is the fifth time organization has been mentioned. "Interpersonal skills" is a perfect opportunity to mention that you've waited tables/worked retail/ done any other jobs with the public.*

- Experience at multitasking while working in a fast-paced environment. *Again, retail and waiting tables would be perfect, especially if you've worked over Christmas.*

- Superior verbal and written communication skills. *You should have some experience with writing in college. If you've ever answered phones or done any public speaking, mention that.*

Please e-mail your cover letter and résumé w/ salary requirements to: XXX, subject line "Subsidiary Rights Position." Résumé submitted without salary requirements will not be considered. *Ouch. I hate this. Do your research. Check out the Publishers Weekly salary survey and other job listings to see if they say how much they pay. Don't shoot for the moon—if your salary requirements are too high, they may assume you won't be happy doing this job for significantly less, and they won't even interview you. But if you lowball yourself, you may dig yourself a hole that's hard to crawl out of. Also, in all applications pay particular attention to any specific directions, such as this note about the subject line. If you don't get that right, you won't get an interview. Instead, you will have just proven you do not pay attention to details.*

JOB LISTING 2

Executive Assistant, Literary Agency
This job will put you on the front lines running a top literary agency from soup to nuts, *This may sound scary, but assistants usually run the office. That's not uncommon.* including foreign rights, audio and first serial rights, managing interns, redlining contracts, working with the bookkeeper and utilizing our software for managing author accounts. *Don't worry, they'll train you on all the above.* Applicants should have made the choice to become a literary agent and want to enter a job that is an intensive training period for becoming one. *This means no wannabe authors for one, and also preferably no wannabe editors. If either of these applies to you, keep*

your mouth shut about it. You should be a voracious, comprehensive reader, have an open mind to all forms of great writing, both contemporary and historical fiction and nonfiction, adult and young adult, *Seriously, you need to have read a lot of books. Expect to be grilled extensively in the interview about what books you've read lately. You ought to be able to name at least ten that have been published in the last three years. And they ought to be in a few different genres. Read up.* and have a creative, entrepreneurial personality. *Not entirely sure what this means. Creative I get, but entrepreneurial is a little trickier. A way to address this would be if you have ever helped start anything. Did you create your own club in college? Were you a charter member of any organization? Did you start a blog or a literary journal? It also may mean being creative at solving problems.* Expert knowledge of Apple computers, website management, social-networking, and Dreamweaver software preferred. *Remember "preferred" never means "required" so don't let a sentence like this stop you from applying. And don't lie about experience you don't have.* A demanding form of multitasking must come naturally to you because of your adept organizational skills. *Ah, more organization, like the last job listing! See a pattern here? You need to be able to juggle multiple tasks and, more important, understand the levels of importance of what needs to be accomplished by the end of each day.* Your writing skills must be top-notch and demonstrate the ability to "pitch" the essence of a book in a sentence as well as write intelligent, inspiring submission letters. *I wouldn't be surprised if they asked you in an interview to "pitch" them a book or two of the ones you've read lately. It really needs to be just one sentence, but it needs to be intriguing and interesting, not just plot. Again, you should have some writing experience from college.* After two years of employment, you will be eligible to attend the London and Frankfurt book fairs. *That will be awesome experience, but it's not really relevant here unless you're unable to travel abroad for some reason.* You must have publishing work experience or be a graduate of one of the college publishing programs. *They say "must" but it isn't true. It's something they'd really like, and it would put you ahead, but you still should apply even without it.*

JOB LISTING 3

Young Readers Sales Division assistant
Our Young Readers Sales Division is seeking an assistant to provide

administrative support *e.g., answering phones, filing, opening mail, etc.* to the Vice President, Director of Field and Mass Merchandise Sales, and the Juvenile Field Sales Force. *This is an assistant to a pretty high-level person. You'd learn a lot, but you'd have limited supervision. Again, you can find out who this is in advance, so start Googling.* This is a great entry level opportunity to liaise with various departments and learn about the business side of the publishing industry! *Notice this is actually the first job that is trying to "sell" itself to you, the applicant, as sales isn't seen as being as glamorous as other departments.*

The Sales Assistant:
1. Maintains and distributes sales materials, seasonally and weekly.
2. Manages Title Information sheets.
3. Distributes materials to trade shows and sales conferences.
4. Manages travel and expense tracking for the department.
5. Processes orders for author appearances.
6. Gathers samples for account presentations.

Guess what? All of the above again means: organization! Pretty basic trafficking and paperwork.

Please apply if you meet the following requirements:

- 4-year college degree or equivalent work experience. *In sales one doesn't always need a college degree, but these days it's more necessary than not.*

- Ability to lift/move packages weighing up to 20 lbs. *Yep, you'll occasionally be schlepping around boxes of books. Think of it as on-the-job weight training. Remember, lift with your legs, not your back.*

- Strong organizational skills and the ability to prioritize multiple assignments. *Hm, this keeps coming up, again and again. What do you think should be repeatedly emphasized in your résumé and cover letter?*

- Excellent written and verbal communication skills. *Again, talk about your writing from college, and for the verbal communication you should address any previous experience where you were dealing with people a lot.*

- Strong follow-up skills and attention to detail. *This is yet another way to say "good organizational skills."*

- Proficiency with Microsoft Office, especially Excel. *You should know enough from school to get by, and the rest you can learn on the job.*

When you're reading through a job listing, you want to be sure that each and every skill, requirement, and attribute they mention is addressed in your material. Often it won't be so obvious on your résumé, which is precisely what your cover letter is for. Never ever let "requirements" hold you back. Worst-case scenario: you won't get the job. But you've got to apply to have a shot.

One friend of mine applied for a job at a publisher that she wasn't remotely qualified for. A day or two later a position two levels down came open at the house. Since her résumé was already in-house, they interviewed her for the lower-level job right away, and she got it. I've never had all of the requirements for any job I've ever had, and yet I got those jobs. On the other hand, I've applied for plenty of jobs where my background couldn't have been more perfect, and I didn't even get an interview, so you've just got to keep plugging away. Just be sure that you tailor every résumé and cover letter to each individual job listing.

Chapter 19

What is the number one piece of advice I can give for getting your résumé in top shape? Proofread! In fact, have several friends proofread it, too, especially your most critical and judgmental friends, anyone who has the nickname "grammar Nazi." Grammar counts, as do spelling and style. Your style needs to be very consistent, including if you end each bullet point with a period or not and the size of your dashes. Yes, they can be different sizes: they are called hyphens, en dashes, and em dashes, but you don't really need to know those particulars, so long as you always use the same ones. Microsoft Word changes them sometimes, so double-check them all at the end, and copy and paste to be sure you've got the same ones everywhere. Proofreading is more important on a publishing résumé than on just about anything else, except maybe a teaching résumé. Be sure your dates are also consistent in placement, formatting, and spacing.

Focus on experience. Unless you're really looking for things to beef up a thin résumé, don't list anything from high school, and don't list any classes. Especially if you were an English major. Unless your major was not in the social sciences, hiring managers can make an educated guess as to what classes you took, and whether you took Chaucer or Shakespeare or Austen isn't relevant. Obviously, if you were a math or science major and now want to go into publishing, you may need to provide a little more explanation as to why, but again, that's what your cover letter is for.

In college you will often gain experiences that are very specific to your school only. You should explain those things, briefly. For instance, my college has eating houses instead of sororities, so after the name of my eating house, I put a comma and then "a women's social and service organization" to explain. We also had our own version of touch football called Flickerball, and I put "touch football" in parenthesis after "Flickerball" to explain. (Why list Flickerball at all? I played for all four years, we were the champions my sophomore year, and team sports show you're good at working in a group.) Most things don't need explanation, but it's good to run your résumé past friends who don't attend your college to be sure those gaps aren't overlooked. On the plus side, unusual items on your résumé tend to be remembered by the interviewer, and also because they're unusual, expect them to come up as interview topics more frequently than they should. This holds true once you've been working for a few years. Currently I have to explain on my résumé what VMR (Vendor Managed Replenishment) and planograms are. It's always good to have at least one proofreader who isn't in your industry.

- Use bullets. Yes, English majors, I know you're more comfortable with paragraphs. Tough. You've got to do it. It is the expected format, and it is easier to read (or skim). You must always have at least two bullets in each section (there's no maximum). That's a grammar rule (from outlines), and if you check my first point up top, grammar is a must here.

- Don't jam in everything possible. Edit. Be judicious if you've been lucky to have a lot of experience, because a page that's absolutely full of information from margin to margin is hard to read. There needs to be white space for the eye to rest, not to mention for the interviewer to write notes. Try to demonstrate some variety in the writing of your résumé, including sentence length.

- Use the same header from your résumé on your cover letter and your list of references. Pretend it's letterhead. This gives you a consistent look and helps if pages get separated. (Do not staple them!)

- Vary your action verbs. Each bullet should start with an action verb, and ideally they'd all be different, although sometimes that's hard. If you must to have two that are the same, be sure they're separated by a few lines. They should be present tense for your current job, past for previous jobs.

- Knowledge of Word, Excel, and Outlook is assumed. But you should list "knowledge of Office, including Publisher, PowerPoint, and Access" if you have that, as those three programs aren't as widely used, but they're certainly needed. Don't worry if you don't have a ton of programs to list here, as most companies use proprietary software that doesn't transfer from one company to another, so they're used to some training.

- Be specific. If you wrote for the student newspaper, tell how often it's published, how many articles you wrote, and what the circulation is. If you were social chair for your fraternity, tell how many members you had and what your budget was. If it's at all possible to add any numbers to your résumé, do it!

- Try different fonts. Don't just use Arial or Times New Roman. In fact, you might use more than one. I use a serif font for my headers, and a sans serif font for my body. A sans serif font is easier to read at a smaller size. A serif is the little tail or curl on the tops and bottoms of letters in fonts such as Times New Roman, Garamond, and Bookman. Sans serif fonts, such as Arial, Verdana, and Calibri, don't have those tails.

What not to do

- Don't use colored paper or colored fonts. That's a bad way to stand out from the crowd.

- Don't think that for an entry-level job you have enough pertinent previous experience to merit a résumé that is more than one page. You do not. One page is all you get.

- Don't say that you have writing experience. That is assumed.

- Don't list foreign languages you aren't fluent in, particularly if you don't plan to use a language in your career (such as looking for books in translation for publication).

- Don't have an objective line. A résumé should be about what you bring to a business, not what the company can do for you. It also feels like filler to beef up a light résumé.

- Don't use the same résumé for every job application. You should tailor each one specifically. Be sure that as many of the points in the job listing are covered as possible (and the rest are covered in your cover letter).

When you have put your résumé through many, many proofreads, convert it to a PDF. That way you don't have to worry about anything getting accidentally deleted or the recipient being able to reveal changes.

Have your list of references ready when you apply. If at all possible, you want your list to include some people who are fairly impressive (or at least have impressive titles). But if you are entry-level, don't be afraid to have a professor on your list, and maybe another officer from your sorority, or a colleague from the honor council or student union board. If you are already working, don't list your current direct supervisor, who you likely don't want to know about your job search. Not only will you have to also list your supervisors on the application—so it's a waste to list them twice—but often the company has a policy that they can only state that yes you worked there, between these dates, and no you weren't fired for cause. So don't list them.

Always ask your references if it's okay to list them so they're not surprised by a call. Also think about who you list—be sure they're people who, if they're surprised, aren't likely to flail and say anything that comes to mind. You want people who are good on their feet, tactful, and who truly respect you and your work. They absolutely can be from other departments. Be sure to confirm how best to contact them.

Timing is everything. The fall is ideal for job hunting. Spring has the maximum number of job lookers competing with you, but in the fall a lot of people quit to go to grad school, so there are more openings.

Do you have something to carry your résumé in? This makes you look more professional and keeps you organized. Office stores stock leatherette folders, which hold a notepad on one side and have a place to slip loose papers on the other.

Don't forget to bring two or three extra copies of your résumé, on nice paper.

Chapter 20

Cover Letters

Your cover letter is the time to showcase the research you've done on the publishing house/imprint/editor/agent. You should be able to name specific books/authors you like that the editor or agent worked with or published. If this publishing house has a particular niche, explain that you know what that is and why you want to work in that genre. Showing that you have done research tells the hiring manager that this isn't a blanket form letter you're sending to everyone. It says that you have targeted them specifically and you truly do like their books, which encourages them to think you'd fit in well. It also shows your research skills and that you're really putting effort into your job hunt. That should translate to a good work ethic once you get a job.

Remember to focus on the job skills the publisher is looking for, not just on what you personally are good at. This is also a good time to honestly assess your strengths and weaknesses and be sure you're working with them, not fighting them. If you really aren't organized, you should think twice before applying for a job that mentions it five times in the description. On the other hand, if you've found methods that work for you—from using checklists to taking extensive notes to using the reminders app on your phone—then you certainly can apply to a job that wants an organized person. In fact, you can even mention a few of the organizational tools you use. But if organizing more than sixty appointments for your boss's trip to the Frankfurt Book Fair is going to drive you insane, reconsider applying.

Your cover letter is also where you explain how seemingly unrelated experience is actually pertinent. This is where you talk about how you gained a lot of communication experience dealing with irate customers at your summer

Learning extrovert skills

In college I was in an eating house (a local social and eating house, similar to a sorority), and I was the kitchen manager of it for two semesters. Mostly thanks to speaking at the house meeting every single week (reminding members of dishwashing duties and letting them know about menu changes), I have zero problems with speaking in front of a large group. This helped me later, as an editor has to present her books to the entire publishing house every season.

Also as an officer I was expected to introduce myself to new members and help them feel at home, which made me very relaxed when later I was professionally networking and meeting agents. As an editor I met, on average, two new agents every week. As a sales rep, I went to twenty-five bookstores every week and met with owners and buyers. Once at sales conference I was asked to give two presentations about my department to over fifty people. I had no idea how much public speaking was a component of publishing, but it is, and that's a skill I developed in college without realizing it. This is an example of a skill necessary to these jobs that isn't one of the first you'd think of. But as it is necessary, it would be a good skill to point out that your competition will likely overlook.

movie theater or theme park job. You can talk about how organized you were while administrating a $40,000 budget for your sorority's social board (not to mention the events you organized). You can discuss how you came up with a new filing system while you were a student assistant in the history department or how you helped the campus bookstore with ordering the textbooks for the new semester (organization, deadlines, and communicating with dozens and dozens of professors and departments—jackpot!). You'll need to think back over your own jobs and experience, pick out the details that apply to this job, and point them out.

Keep in mind your competition. The stereotype of the typical applicant, the liberal arts student, may include being flaky, flighty, and bad with deadlines, as well as being disorganized. Not only will this be the stereotype you'll be fighting, but many of your competitors will have these traits, and you'll want to set yourself apart from them. Be certain to mention any opposing qualities you may have, with concrete examples.

Chapter 21

Informational Interviews

S ometimes it's hard to get a real job interview. There aren't any openings or are openings only for people with experience. But you still need to be finding out more about the industry, getting your face in front of people who can help you get a job, and expanding your industry network. One way to do that is in informational interviews. You can see these as a preliminary step toward an actual job interview and a way to hone your interviewing skills without pressure.

When you find a particular agent or editor or other industry veteran with whom you share many interests, go ahead and contact them directly. You never know if the editor who's worked on five of your favorite authors may have just had an assistant quit. Even if there's not an opening, ask that editor for an informational interview. Their assistant may quit a week from now.

Informational interviews are not a substitute for a real interview, and if you go into one with that attitude, you may well annoy the interviewer and burn a bridge you didn't mean to. With an informational interview, the interviewer doesn't have to read over your résumé beforehand carefully, they don't need to take notes, and they will be a lot less stressed, as they won't be a person short in the office or making time for a half dozen interviews. So the person giving the informational interview will be in a better mood, less rushed, and less anxious. The benefit is that you can learn a lot about the job. The drawback is that there isn't a job available yet!

The other big way an informational interview differs from a job-seeking interview is in the question-and-answer dynamic. In a job-seeking interview, the job seeker (you) will mostly be asked a barrage of questions and will have the chance to ask a couple at the end. In an informational interview, you should be prepared with a few dozen questions, as your queries will steer the conversation. This is your chance to find out everything you ever wanted to know about the business in general, and the publishing house or imprint in particular. You want to ask specific questions regarding these topics, but other great questions to ask are how the interviewer started her career and what led her to her current position and what she loves (and dislikes) about it. In an informational interview, the stakes are so low that her guard will be down, and she'll be much more likely to give you an honest assessment.

You still will need to do a lot of the same prep work already discussed, as you are likely to be asked about what areas of publishing you are interested in, what you like to read, and what draws you to the industry and that particular department. The person you're interviewing with may know about an opening at another publishing house or in another department, so you should not treat this opportunity too casually or indifferently.

After an informational interview, just as with a job-seeking interview, you want to send a follow-up thank-you note. You also want to link to this person through LinkedIn, and down the road, if you run across an article pertinent to a topic you two discussed, send her a copy as a way to stay in touch. In addition to learning about the job responsibilities of a career you are interested in, the other big goal of an informational interview is networking.

Chapter 22

Job Interviews

You've sent out your résumé, complete with a great cover letter, and now you've been asked to come in for an interview. Congratulations! Getting your foot in the door is a huge step. But don't let your guard down. Now is the time to prepare so that you can really shine. Once you get an interview, you have a lot of preparing to do.

First, come up with a list of interview questions you might be asked. Then think about your answers. Then rehearse. Out loud.

The current trend in interviewing is to ask behavioral questions. This means, instead of being asked about your greatest weakness or where you see yourself in five years, you're more likely to be asked to describe a time when you made a mistake in a professional setting and how you resolved it. You should still prepare for the nonbehavioral questions, as many interviewers are not up-to-date on this new technique. Also some interviewers like to ask bizarre questions to throw you off and see how you think on your feet in a high-pressure situation. Those questions don't actually give the interviewer much good information and luckily are very rare, as they're impossible to prepare for.

Behavioral questions can be tough. You should brainstorm some in advance and come up with at least two examples for each of the basic types of questions, as you may be asked the same question a second time with only a minor tweak to the phrasing. Be sure to only use examples where there was a resolution of the situation. If you are a recent college grad, you may not have many examples that happened in a workplace, but it's okay to give examples of similar situations from volunteer work or extracurricular activities. The interview is a great place to show your creativity, by answering such questions with examples from outside the workplace. You can use creating a literary magazine as an example of working with a team to accomplish a goal. An example of creative problem solving could be a time when you suggested a different filing method to the business manager of the campus library, or when you took it upon yourself to write a training manual for new hires at your summer retail job. The interviewer will understand that your previous experience isn't going to be in an office and won't be about going to meetings and running spreadsheet reports. But that doesn't get you out of answering these sorts of questions. Everyone will have had to work with an unpleasant person or an unreasonably demanding boss, even if you were just babysitting.

Next, come up with a list of questions you want to ask in the job interview. Ideally, an interview is a two-way street. You should also use the interview to learn more about the job, what it entails, and if this is a place where you would feel comfortable working. It looks bad if you have no questions, as they will think you are ill-prepared.

Prepare a list of a dozen questions. Expect about half to be answered in the interview; few will prove irrelevant, which will still leave two or three at the end. These should be open-ended questions about the management techniques of the manager, the atmosphere and work environment of the business, and the specifics of working there on a day-to-day basis. Don't come with yes/no questions, and definitely don't ask any questions about salary or benefits until you are offered a job; otherwise you'll look mercenary. Ask for the business cards of everyone you speak with.

Do wear a suit to your interview, or a blazer with a dress for women, even though publishing houses are business casual. You can't go wrong with looking too professional, and if in doubt, go with your more conservative outfit. An interview is not the time to push boundaries. For women, keep your hair back somehow so you don't touch it during the interview. Pay attention to the details and wear nice closed-toed shoes, a watch (even if you don't look at it!), and nice but conservative jewelry (and be sure it doesn't make noises when you gesture, like bracelets that rattle).

If you are interviewing for an editorial position, editors frequently end interviews by handing you a manuscript and asking you to write a reader's report. She wants a half page of description and analysis and then an opinion on whether this book should be bought. The whole reader's report should be just a single page. No more. Try writing one for the next few books you read. All books can, in fact, be boiled down to a one- or-two-sentence plot description. After the plot description, you need to discuss what's good about the book and what's bad. Don't dwell on the minutiae, but instead focus on larger issues, such as:

- Are the characters consistent and three-dimensional?
- Do any important characters not appear until mid-book?
- Is the plot predictable?
- Is the ending adequately satisfying or annoyingly pat?
- Do any important events occur offstage?
- Does the action keep moving or are there any slow parts?

She's certainly not looking for spelling and grammar issues, nor problems with minor details, so ignore those (unless it's a copyediting test, of course). And here's a secret tip: this manuscript she's giving you has already been bought. It doesn't make sense for an editor to assign you a manuscript the editor's not already read, and if she's read it and rejected it, why would she want to keep it hanging around and read another report on why it is bad? The truth is, she's got a book with problems that she's trying to edit, and she's intrigued to see if you've noticed the same editorial issues she has, or different ones, and what exactly they are.

A reader's report doesn't go to the author, so it doesn't need to beat around the bush, and you should write truthfully about what editorial issues you see. Be straightforward and honest.

Finally, you want to analyze the market for this book. Who do you think would buy it? Where would be good places to promote it? Is there a tie-in with a holiday or a season? Does this book have potential to be sold nontraditionally, such as in schools, or in a non-bookstore like Urban Outfitters or Whole Foods? You also want to weigh the book's potential for sales against the amount of work required to get it in saleable condition, and then say if you would personally recommend buying it or not. You will e-mail the report back to the editor in the next couple of days. Be sure to adhere to any deadline you're given for this assignment.

After the interview, you want to think about how it went. Figure out where you had gaps in your knowledge and if there were certain types of questions that flustered you so that you can do better next time. Interviewing is a skill, which means it will improve with practice and effort.

Whatever response time frame the interviewer gives you, double it. Only then should you send a brief follow-up; don't ask directly for a decision, but instead inquire about their time frame for the next steps in the process. Send thank-you notes (see **chapter 28**).

Chapter 23

New York, New York

I f you can go ahead and move to New York to be there for the job hunt, that's your best bet. You can then be available for an interview the next day and able to start a new job immediately. It may be tough financially, but it will almost certainly cut your job-hunt time down substantially. Also, you can start networking in your field in your city, which will help.

When you are applying for a job from out of state, it can be tough. Companies don't want to wait longer than two weeks for you to start, they certainly don't want someone in an entry-level position to even ask about relocation payments, and also they don't know if you're serious about moving or if it's just something you're thinking about. There are ways around these problems. Do you know someone in New York? Will she let you use her address on your résumé? (Out-of-state cell phone area codes are common these days, so that's not a concern.)

If you have a friend in New York, in addition to using his address, you might also make sure you can stay on his sofa when coming into the city for a job interview. Job-hunting expenses, including flights and suits, are tax write-offs, so keep your receipts.

If you can't use another address, explain why you're moving there, how much you really want to move there, and that you're moving whether you get this job or not. You should also mention that you are willing to pay your own relocation costs.

The cost of living in New York is very high, and the low pay in publishing makes that a tough pill to swallow, but getting by is not impossible. You will probably have to move to outside Manhattan; Brooklyn is nearly as expensive as Manhattan these days, so check out Queens and New Jersey. Research the neighborhoods beforehand, as you don't want to get stuck someplace that turns out to be unpleasant. If you have a friend or acquaintance already in the city who can help familiarize you with the neighborhoods, that can be a big help. Roommates are also a help to make the finances work. You may end up far off a subway line, so look for some good walking shoes. My first apartment in Queens was more than a mile from the subway!

Part IV

Nontraditional Paths to Publishing

Don't give up if you don't get your dream job right away. Make the most of your time, find something you like to do, keep reading, freelance if you can, and network as much as possible. This part of the book will give you some ideas about how to put this time to use to make you even more prepared for a job in the publishing world.

Chapter 24

New York Is Not the Center of the Universe,

or … how to get a job in
publishing somewhere else

Yes, the major publishing houses are all located in New York City. Yes, it's exciting to live in the city and good for your career. Yes, it is also expensive, dirty, dangerous, and difficult to live in. If you don't really want to live there, you'd rather be near family, you like a warmer climate, or you've done your five years of experience and want out of the city but not out of publishing, never fear. You have options.

Sales
Sales reps are everywhere and work all over the country and abroad. Please read **chapter 9** about sales for more information.

Smaller Publishers
Please read **chapter 14** about small publishers for more information. Their having fewer employees may make it tough to get a job, but it will also mean less competition for openings. Some larger and midsize publishers that aren't in New York City include:

Algonquin Books: Chapel Hill, North Carolina
Andrews McMeel Universal: Kansas City, Missouri
Baker & Taylor Publishing Group: San Diego, California
Bendon: Ashland, Ohio
Chronicle Books: San Francisco, California
Da Capo Press*: Cambridge, Massachusetts

Dalmatian Press: Franklin, Tennessee
Dover Publications: Mineola, New York
F+W Media: Cincinnati, Ohio, and Avon, Massachusetts
Gibbs Smith Publisher: Layton, Utah
Globe Pequot Press: Guilford, Connecticut
Harlequin*: Toronto, Ontario, Canada
HCI Books: Deerfield Beach, Florida
HighBridge Audio: Minneapolis, Minnesota
Houghton Mifflin Harcourt*: Boston, Massachusetts
John F. Blair Publishers: Winston-Salem, North Carolina
John Wiley & Sons*: Indianapolis, Indiana
McSweeney's: San Francisco, California
Milkweed Editions: Minneapolis, Minnesota
Rodale Books*: Emmaus, Pennsylvania
Running Press: Philadelphia, Pennsylvania
Seal Press: Berkeley, California
Sourcebooks*: Naperville, Illinois
Storey Publishing: North Adams, Massachusetts
Timber Press: Portland, Oregon
Tin House*: Portland, Oregon
Ulysses Press: Berkeley, California
Westview Press: Boulder, Colorado

*They also have offices in New York, so the particular department you want to work in may be in the New York City office.

Nearly every university has a university press, from American University in Washington, D.C., to Vanderbilt University in Nashville, Tennessee. There are also literary agencies, book distributors, and a ton of small publishers not in New York. The list above just barely scratches the surface.

Freelance work

Copyeditors and proofreaders work freelance and live all over the country, as noted in **chapter 5**. You will also find people around the country working as independent editors, agents, ghostwriters, publishing consultants, marketers, and so on. Most of the time these people are former New Yorkers who started out in the publishing industry. Some experience working in New York is generally going to be crucial to success in these kinds of jobs, as one needs both the experience and the contacts.

Wholesalers

There are three major book wholesalers in the United States. Ingram Book Group is located in La Vergne, Tennessee; Baker & Taylor is in Charlotte, North Carolina; and Bookazine is in Bayonne, New Jersey. Wholesalers buy from publishers and sell to retailers. In addition to the job of buyer, they have data entry, legal, finance, sales, account management, and warehouse jobs. Please read **chapter 10** about buying for more information.

Bookselling

Books-A-Million is in Birmingham, Alabama; Hudson Booksellers (in all the airports) is in Marietta, Georgia; and Amazon is in Seattle, Washington. Additionally every chain store that sells books has a book buyer. Being a buyer at a major retailer usually involves other responsibilities but is another option for jobs outside of New York City. For example, Kmart is near Chicago, Illinois; Target is in Minneapolis, Minnesota; Lowe's Home Improvement is in Mooresville, North Carolina; PetSmart is in Phoenix, Arizona; and Office Depot is in Boca Raton, Florida.

And there are even more options. There are regional independent bookselling associations, publications like BookPage (based in Nashville), and buyers at large independent bookstores. Author escorts in major media markets (no, not that kind of escort!) are media professionals who drive authors to events and sometimes book media events.

So while New York can be exciting and fun, if it's not for you, don't despair. There are other options.

Chapter 25

Experience

Don't discount your previous experience, even if it seems unrelated. Through my bartending and TicketMaster jobs, I became extremely diplomatic and not easily insulted. I also learned that I work just fine in high-pressure situations. These were very useful skills in publishing.

For jobs in marketing, publicity, and even sales, skills are very transferable from one industry to another. There are certainly quirks to the publishing industry, but having worked in marketing previously will give you a leg up on a publishing marketing job, even without publishing experience.

In college, if your school has a writing center, try to become an instructor. Nothing teaches better editing skills than reading a lot of bad writing. You can also work on editing skills through websites like Swoon Reads. Swoon Reads is a division of Macmillan actively looking for outside readers to read and vote on which of their young adult romance manuscripts should be published. Websites featuring works-in-progress like Wattpad also need readers and critiquers.

You can work or volunteer at a library. Libraries are a giant customer of publishers, and it will keep you abreast of what's currently being published and what the issues are in that area of the book business. Bestselling books in bookstores aren't exactly the same as the top circulating books in libraries, and it's interesting to see the differences. Libraries are a vital force in communities, and they do have an impact on book publishing, even if it's not as obvious as bookstores' influence. If a major library system buys a book, it can not only be as big a sale as a chain bookstore's purchase, but libraries don't return books to publishers like bookstores do.

If you work at a bookstore (see **chapter 11**), try to gain skills beyond shelving, such as helping with the store's social media, writing articles for the newsletter, or organizing and leading a book discussion group. You can help with events, work in shipping and receiving, or try your hand at coming up with merchandising ideas.

If you do none of the above but have a completely nonbook job, volunteer with a literacy nonprofit like firstbook.org. Volunteer to be a reading buddy at schools to help at-risk kids or ESL kids. Or start a book club in your neighborhood.

You can try to find work as a reviewer for publications like *BookPage* or *Publishers Weekly*, or you can start a book blog. Posting your own book reviews shows your critical-thinking skills about books. It can also show publishers that you can write and that you are thoughtful, with high editorial standards, and are widely read. Content from your own blog can demonstrate your ability to come up with good ideas, execute them well, keep followers engaged, expand your readership base, and write content. It shows you're serious about books. You would need to maintain it well, so if you post only a couple of times and then drop it, do not mention it in any job application. Don't fill it with memes—you want mostly original content, showing your creativity and curiosity. You can go with a gimmick—there have been book bloggers who aim to read a particular list of award winners or who plan to read a book a day for a year, but that can prove harder than you think when you start out, so be careful to not pick a goal you can't maintain.

This type of experience will help if you are looking for a job in marketing, which could entail maintaining content on the publisher's website, including a blog or newsletter. It may also give you exposure to publicists, marketers, and authors, who will approach you to review their books. If you follow through and actually give well-reasoned and creative reviews of their books, you can develop relationships.

There are always things you can do to boost your book-related experience on your résumé: you can join organizations, such as the Women's National Book Association (WNBA)—which isn't just for women—the Jane Austen Society of North America (JASNA), the Edith Wharton Society, the National James Baldwin Literary Society, the William Faulkner Society, the Cormac McCarthy Society, the World Science Fiction Society, Sisters in Crime, the Academy of American Poets, PEN/American (particularly good if you're interested in international literature/literature in translation), or whatever sort of literary organization excites you.

Once you join, you can add both your local and national groups to your

LinkedIn profile. On my résumé I have a section called "Organizations" where I have WNBA listed, as well as JASNA and YPG (the Young to Publishing Group). Then, if there is a local chapter, go to the meetings. Meet the other members. This is where you start networking.

Networking with my mom

Back when I was working at Bookstar in shipping and receiving, I was pretty unhappy. I was broke and at a loss for what to do next. I was even considering graduate school.

My mother is a long-time member of JASNA (the Jane Austen Society of North America). I joined after I took a senior seminar on Jane Austen in college, but I was a member only in name and never went to the meetings.

Then one day my mother was at a meeting and someone politely asked after her children. Mom told her I was working at Bookstar but looking for another job. *Didn't she go to Davidson College?* someone asked. Susie, a new member, had been very interested in this otherwise innocuous conversation. She was the head of the Big Eight (now Big Five) department in buying at Ingram Book Group. She had an opening and had just been told that instead of hiring someone with either a degree or experience, she had to hire someone with both. Now she'd just heard about someone at a bookstore with a degree from Davidson who was looking for another job. She interrogated my mother after the meeting, who got her contact information. I was interviewing with Susie less than a week later (of course, during the interview we discussed which Jane Austen movie adaptations we liked best), and I was working for her in less than a month.

This goes to show that these literary/publishing organizations can be great sources for jobs. Networking is essential, even if sometimes it comes through your parents.

Chapter 26

Publishing Programs

Many people coming straight out of college think a good way to get into publishing is ... more college! There are a few publishing programs around the country, such as those at Emerson College in Massachusetts, Pace University in New York, the City College of New York, Columbia University, NYU, the University of Denver in Colorado, George Washington University in Washington, D.C., and DePaul University in Chicago. But are they worth the money and time? They can give you valuable networking opportunities, but in trade publishing, additional education beyond a BA is unnecessary. Only a quarter of people working in publishing have a graduate degree and hardly any of them, except the lawyers and MBAs, ever use them. A graduate degree is more useful if you plan on working in academic, textbook, and reference publishing.

I knew a couple of editorial assistants who did the full NYU or Columbia publishing programs. For someone with zero contacts and no networking options who's had no luck with applying for jobs, it can be a great way to make contacts in the industry (the New York programs are probably best for this). It also can get something publishing-related on your résumé, if you are unsure how else to do so. Most people end up with a certificate, but you can even get a master's in some programs.

A lot of the information in these classes you learn on the job. For instance, I don't think editing can really be taught. It's mostly learned by watching others do it, by reading editors' editorial letters, and by looking through edited manuscripts. That is why the job of editor is basically set up as an apprenticeship. And at a large publishing house, while it's good to work with other departments, it's not crucial for an editor to know much about publicity, and vice versa. (At a small house, it could be much more helpful, as there will be more overlap between departments.)

Publishing programs can certainly be a foot in the door but it's no guarantee. It doesn't exempt anyone from having to do the heavy lifting of job hunting. And if you think the networking gives you a lock on future job opportunities, remember that there are only a handful of professors and scores of students trying to use those few professors' contacts for job leads.

I did take a few courses in publishing programs. I waited until I already had a job as an editorial assistant and could better judge which classes would be the most useful. I took three classes at NYU: the Business of Publishing, Publishing Law, and Copyediting. The first two were incredibly helpful, and the last one was helpful years later when I began freelance editing. The Business of Publishing helped me understand P&Ls, or profit and loss statements, which must be filled out for every book before it's bought. Publishing Law helped me understand not just contracts better but also permissions, libel, and copyright, all of which came up from time to time, and it was very nice that I felt comfortable and like I could handle a fairly complicated topic. Copyediting is helpful only if you plan to do copyediting.

One view on publishing programs

As I was looking into various publishing programs, graduate school and continuing ed, I realized that while I knew a little bit about it, I had a friend, Emily Sachs, who went for the whole shebang and got a master's in publishing. Emily is production coordinator at a high-powered government contractor in the D.C. metro area that specializes in developing and delivering all kinds of training—instructor-led, web-based, blended—and in conducting human capital analysis. She also is a past president of the Washington, D.C. chapter of the Women's National Book Association.

I asked Emily a few questions about her experience.

When and where did you go to school, and what degree did you receive?
I attended Pace University in New York City from 2003 to 2005 and received a master of science in publishing.

Has the information you learned at Pace been helpful to you in your career?
In my opinion, no education is a wasted experience. With that said, I feel as if I learned more valuable lessons by doing, rather than by sitting in a class-

room. For instance, the book production class, in which we visited presses and production offices and saw people on the job, was more valuable in furthering my education and love of production processes than a classroom scenario.

What was the most helpful thing you learned (or most helpful class)? The least helpful?

The most helpful class was on book design and production. This class taught us the basics about paper, ink, binding, presses, and the design process. Since I wanted to be on the production side of publishing, this was the most interesting class!

The least helpful thing conveyed was that you pick one path—editing or production, book or magazine—and from then on, that is the path you are on, that it is hard to switch over. Many professors at Pace imposed this viewpoint on us. But I have found that this simply isn't true. In my career so far, I have worked for a literary journal, an industry newsletter, a magazine, and a niche book publishing company.

I remember one professor saying repeatedly, "None of you will work in trade book publishing. None of you will make any money. None of you will work in fiction." When students talked about this with our thesis advisor, she shrugged it off: "Oh, that's just how Professor So-and-So is." Although, in fact, I didn't want to work in fiction or in trade book publishing, these exchanges bring up a complaint about Pace. Not only did the faculty have no faith that any of us would "break in," but they didn't go out of their way to assist students in finding jobs in the industry. Students were more helpful than faculty members or the internship coordinator in helping other students to network and find jobs.

Do you think these programs are better for people who aspire to work in publishing and haven't yet or for people already with jobs in the industry?

Everyone has a different reason for advancing his or her education. I am not sure that one can evaluate for whom these programs work better. I attended graduate school right after undergraduate. I always aspired to have a career in publishing when I "grew up" because I wanted to work hands-on producing the written word. I don't work in publishing in the traditional sense; however, I have used both classroom and real-world experience in my career. I never realized that this type of production work was a career path. The company for which I work publishes every day. From instructor guides, to participant manuals, to webinars and proposals, we publish materials that other people consume. I think there is a broader range to what publishing means than was taught in the classroom at Pace.

What do you know now that you most wish you'd known when you were first starting out in this business? Do you have any advice for young adults wanting to break into the book industry?

Education only takes you so far. Real-world experience is every bit as valuable as academic knowledge and is valued more by most prospective employers. Employers look for people with a good work ethic and experience. I don't think my master's degree has given me an advantage when it comes to getting hired, although my on-the-job experience has. My advice to those just starting out would be to apply for internships, part-time jobs, or full-time jobs while you are in school. Join organizations. Volunteer at events within the industry. It is good to have connections in the field in which you want to work.

Can you explain what a production coordinator does?

A production coordinator plans and implements the entire production life cycle, including graphics, desktop publishing, editing, and logistics for all client deliverables. The production team, as a whole, touches everything before it leaves the office: proposals, marketing collateral, and project deliverables, including storyboards, instructor manuals, and participant guides.

A differing view on publishing programs

by Melanie Mitzman, Imprint Marketing Manager at Gallery Books, an imprint of Simon & Schuster

Getting into publishing isn't easy, and sometimes finding publishing as an option can be even harder. While earning my undergraduate degree in print journalism at American University in Washington, D.C.—a track that is heavy in writing, editing, and communicating—never once did a professor or career counselor say to me, "Did you ever consider publishing as a career path?" Even more insulting was that I was a literature minor. So when people ask me how I ended up in publishing, I find there is no short answer, as my path was far from simple.

My road to publishing included (but was not limited to) a stint at a law firm, two layoffs, a massive pay cut to break into trade publishing, moving between trade and academic, and earning a master of science in publishing at Pace University in New York.

There were many other experiences along the way, but earning my MS in publishing was one of my most valuable. When I began my program in 2010, I had also just started a position as a publishing coordinator at an imprint in Perseus Books Group. That job required me to wear many hats, work on multiple projects, and send and receive two hundred–plus emails a day—all of which was done with only three other people on my team. It was a lot to handle, and I easily found myself getting caught in the minutiae of the day.

Though it was overwhelming to start my master's simultaneously with a new position, it improved my overall skill set tremendously. It allowed me to take a step back from my daily work and understand how my role fit into the larger picture of the publishing business. It also helped me understand areas of the industry with which I was less familiar, strengthening my communication with other departments in order to work more efficiently with them. I believe it also made me a stronger candidate for that position and others I've taken since I began the graduate program.

My master's program also provided me with essential networking opportunities without which I would not be where I am today. My publishing coordinator position was eventually promoted to manager, but in June 2012 I was told that my imprint was shutting down and that I would have my job only until August. I was devastated but knew I needed to take immediate action. My first initiative was to create a LinkedIn profile and connect with all of my colleagues and graduate school classmates. I also set up a meeting with one of my professors to get advice on what to do, and she encouraged me to utilize my Pace contacts.

This was a key piece of advice that led to a job offer with Oxford University Press just four days before my last at Perseus Books Group. I had contacted a classmate with whom I had had a few classes during my time at Pace. She told me about a job opening and strongly rallied for me to the hiring manager. Without her I may not have been able to get beyond the "black hole" of human resources—or get a job as quickly as I needed.

The connections people make with classmates in a graduate program can be essential. In a graduate program for publishing, it can be life changing. The people who are in classes together often go on to recommend one another, work together, and hire one another. They are classmates who potentially become colleagues, clients, or even bosses. The publishing industry is small, and people often stay in it for years and decades. Being in a graduate program for publishing means you're all in it together. There's a certain camaraderie that I don't assume exists in many other programs. It's a "book nerds unite" type of attitude, and it can provide a wonderful advantage for people just joining the industry.

It has taken me several jobs, bosses, companies, and years to be in a place where I feel truly satisfied with the work I'm doing, the people I work with, and the books I work on. Though I experienced setbacks over time, I took many steps forward to get to where I am today, and I feel a giant step was enrolling in a publishing graduate program. Sure, it's certainly not for everyone—the money alone can be a serious deterrent. But publishing is first and foremost about passion, and just as it takes an immense amount of passion to get a book from just an idea to the shelves of a bookstore, it takes even more to make it in publishing.

Chapter 27

Internships

An internship is a short-term position that may be paid and gives a taste of what a particular business or organization is like. Some internships are just one day a week for a few months. Others are full-time for anywhere from two months to a year. Some college career centers will help students secure internships. In other situations you'll have to find and apply for internships on your own.

Some interns complain that all they do is answer phones, get coffee, and run errands, and therefore, how is this supposed to be experience for "a real job"? Well, wake up, that is a real job! At my first job in publishing in New York as an editorial assistant for the head of an imprint, my primary responsibilities were ... answering the phones, sorting the mail, watering the plants, keeping the office fully stocked with supplies, fixing paper jams in the printer, making appointments and lunch reservations for my boss, and other menial tasks. Interns aren't given menial tasks just because they are menial, and certainly no one wants to deny interns from gaining "real" experience, but menial tasks are in fact a large component of the job of an assistant in publishing.

Yes, it would be great if you'd get to do some "real" work along with the mundane office tasks. That may require some initiative on your part, but it should be part of your responsibilities. For an unpaid internship, the company is legally required to teach you, and that means not just giving you mundane tasks. If the internship is paid, those requirements are lifted. Not every company is aware of the legal requirements of internships, and while you are well within your rights to point them out, you likely will not get the result you're looking for.

Unless you have a very conscientious and thoughtful boss, you might have to approach him and ask for more responsibility, ask to work on a project you find interesting, or offer to do a task you've seen is necessary in the office. Not only will many bosses appreciate your asking—it shows your interest and enthusiasm and relieves him of having to constantly think of something for you to do—but taking initiative is a personality trait highly valued in prospective job candidates, so you want it to be a word that will immediately come to mind when your internship boss is called to provide a reference for you. If your boss truly is too busy to give you tasks, ask the other people in the office. They will usually be happy to have someone who can help out a little bit, and the more people you work with during your internship, the better, as those are more people you can ask to be a reference.

The Association of American Publishers (AAP) lists publishing internship contacts, including small publishers and agencies, as well as the big houses. Look for internships that offer a variety of experience, a paycheck, college credit, and/or flexible hours (so you can get a paying job as well), like Hachette (in Boston and Nashville, as well as New York, and theirs are paid), HarperCollins (this is my favorite internship, as they actually rotate you through a variety of departments, so you get a rounded education in the industry as well as many more networking contacts), Macmillan, Penguin (paid!), Random House, and Simon & Schuster. One thing to keep in mind: internships aren't closed to you after you've graduated. You can intern the following summer. As there are more job openings in the fall than the spring anyway, this would postpone your serious job search until when there are the most openings.

And most major publishers still have a travel division, despite declining sales. Travel books are mostly annuals, so they come out in the very early part of the year. Which means fall is crazy busy in that department, but obviously spring and summer wouldn't be, so they need seasonal help every fall, which is normally filled with an intern. If you go to a college where you have flexibility in your schedule, you can be at a huge advantage, as fall and spring internships often have very little competition.

Be creative. Approach a smaller publisher or agency or editor in your area and ask if they've considered having an intern. You might be able to combine both and have an internship where you go to the office just one day a week and do other work at home, allowing you to have a full-time paid job as well.

After your internship has ended, write your boss a (handwritten but legible) thank-you note. Be sure to link to all the people you met through LinkedIn.

Internships are by no means necessary to a future job in publishing (I didn't have one), but they can be a major help, particularly with networking. If you get an internship and can afford it, take it. In the long run, it'll be a bigger help than an unrelated hourly job, even if the pay is a lot less.

Chapter 28

Thank-You Notes

One of the most important things you can do in the job search process is write thank-you notes. I personally hate them: I don't write them for Christmas and birthdays like I should, but you absolutely must for a job interview. For the best impression, a thank-you note must be handwritten legibly (if you are applying for the job of someone's assistant, you will be taking phone messages for them, which is normally done by hand, and they will look to see if your handwriting is readable). Look for something nice like Crane's notepaper (nothing too funky or overly cutesy), and send out your note the same day.

If you have a follow-up or second interview, often just a couple of days after the first, you want them to have already received your note. When you're going for an informational interview and are hoping to come back to this person in a few months to ask them if they know of a job opportunity, absolutely you need for your interviewer to have gotten a prompt thank-you from you.

Yes, these days it is okay to send your follow-up thank-you via e-mail, but that's not as welcome as a paper one. It's easy for an e-mail to get lost amid the hundreds of e-mails editors get daily and even easier for it to be deleted. Personal mail is so rare these days that it is noticed. In more technical fields, an e-mailed thank-you is preferred, but as book publishing is a rather antiquated industry (we are after all producing a product invented more than five hundred years ago), paper is still good here. Do not do both, as you'll seem desperate and needy.

Keep the note short. Be sure to mention some kind of follow-up from the interview itself, whether you bought and are reading a book they recommended, or simply something additional you thought of since the interview. It shouldn't be so generic that they can't connect you to the thank you without referencing your name.

Part V

So you've finally landed

a job in publishing.

Congratulations!

Some Tips Just for the Women

Book publishing is an industry dominated by women, yet men are still paid more and dominate the executive positions at publishing houses. Women need to be prepared for the realities of the workplace, and I hope more women will step up and take on management positions and positions of power. I was lucky to work under a female publisher, because they are rare.

I never read business books, but I picked up *Nice Girls Don't Get the Corner Office: 101 Unconscious Mistakes Women Make That Sabotage Their Careers* by Lois P. Frankel. That evening, I flipped through it, just to see what it was like. I read the whole thing in one night, and I learned several things that I still pay attention to today. These are three things I stopped doing cold turkey:

- Never play with your hair at work. Invest in bobby pins if it really is driving you crazy. Playing with your hair is a flirting sign, even if you don't mean it to be.

- Never sit on your leg. You don't always need to have both feet planted on the floor, but sitting on one leg is infantilizing. It sends the message that you are a child.

- Never refer to yourself as a "girl." This tip is right in the title. The reason nice girls don't get the corner office? Because nice *women* get the corner office.

This book also has quizzes and sidebars that make it an easier read than the majority of business books. Now, I am still working on some of her tips, like not asking so many questions. Especially when there isn't actually a question in the situation. For example, when I was in sales, I shouldn't have asked my boss's permission to make minor decisions about my accounts. Of course I should have told my boss where I was on issues, but by asking him if my decisions were okay, I undermined my authority. This book has great advice I wish I'd read when I was just starting in the business world, and it was recently rereleased in an updated edition.

Another great book for women embarking on their careers is *Lean In: Women, Work, and the Will to Lead* by Sheryl Sandberg. She points out things women (including herself) do to sabotage our own careers, thanks to the way girls are brought up differently, including not speaking up, sitting in the back of the room or not at the table, and not volunteering for new opportunities but instead waiting for someone to bring them to you. This book also would be interesting for men who wish to have equal partnerships and marriages, to learn more about priorities, trade-offs, and dynamics. The new edition, *Lean In: For Graduates*, has even more pertinent advice for women starting their careers.

Are You New? Join the Young to Publishing Group.

I moved to New York and became an editorial assistant in 2000. Luckily, that same year the AAP (American Association of Publishers) started YPG, the Young to Publishing Group. Apparently a lot of people move to New York to be an editor but quit and leave within five years. That's not very efficient, and the AAP wants more of their young people to stick around, so they have a Recruit and Retain department, and the YPG was their brilliant brainstorm.

You need to network. It doesn't matter what department you are in, but if you are new to publishing, you need friends! You need to be able to commiserate, gossip, network, and also have friends to go out with who are on similarly terrible budgets. If things go south at your current job—new boss, layoffs, change in direction, merger, imprint eliminated—you need people you can call on who can help you get interviews, tell you about job openings before they are listed, and act as references. Also, being involved in an organization dedicated to helping improve your career is a good thing to list on your résumé. You don't have to join the board (unless you want to!); there are tons of fun things to participate in with YPG. They have a book-to-film club, a literacy outreach program, a book club, and events from a spelling bee to a "dudes" drinks night to BEA (Book Expo America) on a Boat.

I wish I could still go to YPG events! Of course, I've now been in the book business much longer than five years, not to mention I am not in NYC. But I am thrilled I was able to be a member while I was there. And all newcomers to the industry should join. It gave me a great start.

Once you've landed a job in publishing, you may find yourself job hunting again in a few years. You may have figured out that your work situation is less than ideal. There are some bad bosses out there, bad coworkers, and just plain bad situations. While it is best to try to deal straightforwardly with unfortunate situations and try your hardest to do an excellent job, sometimes you don't have a lot of choice and need to start looking for another job. You don't need to put up with a boss from hell.

Sometimes you need to look for another job because that's the only way to get promoted. Some departments and some managers just don't ever promote from within (or if they do, it's on a much longer time frame, and the pay increase won't be as much as if you were hired elsewhere). A lot of companies put a premium on varied experience across several businesses.

And you might be forced onto the job market due to consolidation and layoffs. The good news is that while there are always mergers at the top of the publishing food chain, there are always start-ups at the bottom, too. The number of books being published isn't decreasing.

Because you will be job hunting at various times throughout your career, it's important to maintain your network, keep your résumé updated, keep your ears open for availabilities, and also help out your own network when you know about openings. Someone who owes you a favor can be invaluable later.

The Young to Publishing Group

Initially I went to YPG's Brown Bag Lunches. These were all at HarperCollins in my day, and they had big-name speakers, including publishers, vice presidents, and department heads, talk about their own early days in the business and how they got to where they are now. Personally, one of the most interesting and funny was a woman from my own company, Alison Lazarus, who talked about her first job at Playboy Books! It was amazing and inspiring to see and hear these important publishing figures talk to us assistants, and it did make me think that maybe one day I could be one of them.

Not only did I learn a lot at these Brown Bag Lunches, but after several months of going, I got an intriguing e-mail—my regular attendance had been noted, and because of my obvious interest in YPG, I was being invited to join the board.

As YPG at the time was still in formation, I got to decide the way in which I wanted to help and pick my title! I was CoChair of New Chapters. We started chapters in Boston and San Diego. We planned events and socials, reached out to speakers, went to book-related plays (like *Wicked*), and gossiped. I made friends at S&S, Harper, Penguin, and several other publishing houses. At least a half dozen of these people I am still friends with today. Naturally, since I am no longer in New York, most of them I keep up with via Facebook, LinkedIn, and blogs, but YPG did give me lifelong friends and business contacts—which is precisely what it is designed for. Oh, and did I mention that it is free?

A Glossary of Publishing Terms

In an interview, it's good if you can throw in a bit of insider lingo. It shows you have been doing your research and are informed about the industry. At the very least, it's good if you can understand what your interviewer is saying to you! Like all industries, publishing has a lot of its own language and abbreviations. This is just a cursory list of some really basic terms that you might not know. Not all of these terms are in this book, but you might run across them in a job listing or conversation.

Advance Reader's Copy—also ARC, or Advance Reader's Edition, or ARE. A prepublication printing of a book made from the second-pass pages (so it will have a few typos as it hasn't had a final proofread, but it will be cleaner than a galley) created for reviewers and other promotions, to feed interest upon publication. The front will usually have what looks like a cover, but the spine will often be plain, and the back cover is a reproduction of the catalog page, with information about publicity and sales.

back copy—any copy that appears on the back of a book. On the hardcover it could be blurbs, quotes, or an excerpt. On the paperback, it's the description, author biography, and quotes.

backlist—older books that are anywhere from three to six months past publication to currently out of print. Backlist are often the bread-and-butter books that pay the bills at a publishing house, such as *What to Expect When You're Expecting*, *Joy of Cooking*, *Little House on the Prairie*, and *Guns, Germs, and Steel*. The books have long since earned out their advances and have proven consistent sellers without any additional marketing or advertising dollars spent on them.

blurb—a quote solicited from a published author or another big-name person in the industry or media to be printed on or in the book as a recommendation.

board book—a format used primarily in children's books. The pages are actually hard cardboard, which means there are very few, and a baby can chew on the pages without immediate disintegration.

children's/adult—notice that *children's* is plural and possessive while *adult* is singular. Yes, this is completely inconsistent and yet it's the conventional reference for each of the segments of publishing.

face out/spine out—how books are shelved at a bookstore. Face out is showing the cover; spine out shows just that: the book's spine. Face-out books sell better, but you can fit a lot more books on the shelf spine out.

flap copy—the description, author biography, and quotes that appear on the inside flaps of a hardcover book.

first and second serial—the rights to print an excerpt of a book in a magazine or newspaper. First serial comes out before the book is published and second serial is any excerpt after the book is published.

frontlist—the brand-new books, published within the last three months.

format—the binding of a book. The most common formats are hardcover, trade paperback, mass market paperback, audio, board book, e-book, and reinforced binding for libraries.

galley—a prepublication printing of a book traditionally made from the first-pass pages or copyedited manuscript (so it will be riddled with typos, as it hasn't been proofread). Sometimes this has a paper or otherwise plain cover. Like an ARC, this is created for prepublication publicity opportunities, such as blurbs and long-lead reviews. Galleys are made as early as possible for books that the publishing house is putting extra effort into promoting. For very high-profile books, ARCs will likely follow.

genre—the subject or category the book belongs in, such as literary fiction, memoir, history, or young adult. More specifically, when people talk about "genre books," they mean adult fiction books that fall into one of these categories: mystery, thriller, romance, Western, science fiction, or fantasy.

imprint—a smaller division of a publishing house. Often these exist to group books according to category or series, such as For Dummies (Wiley) Fodor's Travel Guides (Random House), and Red Dress Ink (Harlequin). Other times they've been ways to reward editors who've done well at a house, and these divisions, while without specific genre affiliations, will usually reflect the personality and interests of the publisher at the helm. Some of the most well-known editor-helmed imprints include Spiegel & Grau, Reagan Arthur Books, and Margaret K. McElderry Books. There can be dozens upon dozens of imprints at a single publishing house.

ISBN—International Standard Book Number. Don't say "ISBN number" as that's repetitive. They are now thirteen digits, with the first three being 978 or 979. The next digit is a 0 or 1, as it indicates the language (English). The next two to four digits are specific to the publisher. The last digit is a check digit that is calculated based on an algorithm of the previous twelve numbers. Supposedly they are all unique, and each format/edition gets a new ISBN, but occasionally a mistake occurs, resulting in a duplication. ISBNs are created by a company called Bowker, and publishers have to purchase ISBNs.

ladder—when the end of two or more consecutive lines is a hyphen or dash. Similar to stacks.

mass market—the smallest size paperback book, also called "rack size." In addition to being sold at bookstores, these books are usually sold at grocery stores, drug stores, airport stores, and mass market retailers like, Kmart. Frequently they are displayed in a metal rack instead of on a shelf like in a traditional bookstore. (*See* premium paperback).

new adult—a brand-new genre that brings YA-type characters into their early twenties. Often has a lot of sexual content.

one-off—a product that is out of the ordinary for an imprint or department's specialty such as a cookbook imprint publishing a memoir or a children's department publishing an adult book.

orphans—three characters or fewer falling on a line by themselves. Production editors eliminate these when possible. Similar to widows.

Out of Print—also called OP. This status code means that a publisher has run out of stock and does not intend to reprint. Technically this indicates that a book's rights have been (or are able to be) reverted back to the author or original publisher. However, it is also often used when rights are retained.

Out of Stock Indefinitely—also called OSI or Permanently Out of Stock. A publisher uses this status code when they have run out of stock, do not intend to print more, but do not want to revert the rights back to the author. As far as the bookselling/buying public is concerned there is no real difference between OP and OSI.

premium paperback—this format is a recent development, basically a slightly taller, slightly more expensive mass market.

Print on Demand—also called POD. A method of printing where a publisher creates an electronic file of a book, which can be printed singly for individual copies, instead of stocking large quantities of a title in a warehouse. Some bookstores have machines, such as an Espresso, and can print POD books right there in about ten minutes. Publishers may also have contracts with Ingram's Lightning Source or other distribution services to keep books available through POD. When a customer orders a book, the order is sent to the POD printer, who prints the requested number of copies and ships the order. POD books often cost a few dollars more than standard printing, but when demand has dropped off significantly, making a book OP is the alternative for most publishers.

running heads—the text at the very top of the page. It can be the book title, author's name, chapter title, or any combination of these.

SASE—Self-Addressed Stamped Envelope. These are mostly going out of style as submissions shift to online-only, but for Luddites, they're still around. Writers will include an SASE with their printed and mailed submission so that the publisher can return an answer to them with minimal effort.

shelf talker—usually a piece of cardstock that is creased in the middle, so half of it can sit on a shelf under books (to hold it in place) while the remainder hangs down over the edge of the shelf. It can either have publisher-produced copy on it, or bookstores can write their own content, such as for "Staff Recommends" displays.

slush—unsolicited manuscripts sent by hopeful writers to editors and agents.

stacks—when the first or last word of three or more consecutive lines is the same. Stacks make the text hard to read, and the reader may end up rereading the same line when there is a stack in the text. Similar to a ladder.

strippable—most mass market and premium mass market books, along with select trade paperback books, are strippable. This is indicated by a triangle with an S in it somewhere on the cover; the triangle should also have a barcode next to it. When a book has run its course in a bookstore and needs to be removed to make room for new books, instead of shipping it back to the publisher for resale (which is cost prohibitive on such low-priced books), the front cover is ripped off and only those covers are returned to the publisher for credit. The rest of the book is trashed or recycled. If you see books for sale without a front cover, those are stolen goods.

subsidiary rights—rights in addition to initial publication that are sold off to other companies, such as serial rights for magazines and newspapers, audiobook licensing, British and translation rights, dramatic rights, and large-print book rights. Please see **chapter 3** about working in subrights for a fuller explanation.

trade paperback—the largest size paperback. This encompasses all paper-back books that aren't mass markets.

trade publishing—publishing that is focused on regular readers at standard bookstores, as opposed to specific publishing, such as professional, technical and reference (PTR); academic; textbooks; and Christian publishing. Some university press books are for a trade audience; some are only for an academic audience.

widows—a line at the top of a page that is not a full-length line. Production editors try to eliminate these where possible to improve readability. Similar to orphans.

Young Adult—also known as YA, these are books for teenagers. While there can be some significant overlap with Middle Reader books, what usually makes a book "young adult" is some kind of risky or controversial content: sex, drugs, alcohol, death, illness (mental or physical), divorce, and so on.

Resources

The first two websites you should go to:

www.linkedin.com Here you will build a profile and link to as many people you know as you can. Don't limit your network, because you don't know where connections may be made.

www.askamanager.org Alison Green gives great advice on job hunting, résumé writing, cover letters, interviews, and references, and then she gives advice on proper behavior at a job, including dealing with difficult coworkers and bosses, how to approach uncomfortable conversations, and when it's time to start looking for another job.

Publishers' websites with job postings

The Big Five

hachettebookgroup.com/about_careers.aspx (Hachette Book Group)
simonandschuster.biz/careers (Simon and Schuster)
harpercollinscareers.com/careers/careers/cr_index.html (HarperCollins)
us.macmillan.com/splash/careers.html (MacMillian Publishers)
us.penguingroup.com/static/pages/aboutus/jobopportunities.html (Penguin)
careers.randomhouse.com (Random House)
Random House and Penguin are in the process of merging but as of the time of this printing, they had not yet combined their websites or job listings.

Midsize publishers

amuniversal.com/amu/AMU_Careers.htm (Andrews McMeel Universal)
chroniclebooks.com/our-company/jobs/openings (Chronicle Books)
doverpublications.com/jobs (Dover Publications)
fwmedia.com/careers (F+W)
harlequin.com/articlepage.html?articleId=921&chapter=0 (Harlequin)
careers.hmhco.com (Houghton Mifflin Harcourt)
gpp.iapplicants.com (Globe Pequot Press)
groveatlantic.com (Grove Atlantic)
mheducation.com/careers (McGraw Hill)

perseusbooksgroup.com/perseus/employment.jsp (Perseus Books)
routledge-ny.com/info/careers (Routledge)
scholastic.taleo.net/careersection/2/jobsearch.ftl?lang=en (Scholastic)
wiley.com/WileyCDA/Section/id-311100.html (John Wiley)
workman.com/about/career (**Workman**)
books.wwnorton.com/books/jobs (W. W. Norton)

Some major agencies

Abrams Artists Agency

Aitken Alexander Associates

Andrea Brown Literary Agency

Blauner Books Literary Agency

Curtis Brown

Darhansoff & Verrill

Dunow, Carlson & Lerner Literary Agency

Dystel & Goderich Literary Management

Folio Literary Management

Foundry Literary + Media

Greenburger Associates

Harold Ober Associates

Harvey Klinger

ICM Partners

InkWell Management

Irene Skolnick Literary Agency

Jane Rotrosen Agency

Janklow & Nesbit Associates

Jean V. Naggar Literary Agency

Jennifer Lyons Literary Agency

Kneerim, Williams & Bloom

Levine Greenberg Literary Agency

Linda Chester Literary Agency

Liza Dawson Associates Literary Agency

McCormick & Williams

Regal Literary

Sandra Dijkstra Literary Agency

Scovil Galen Ghosh Literary Agency

Susan Golomb Literary Agency

The Susan Rabiner Literary Agency

Trident Media Group

William Morris Endeavor

Writers House

The Wylie Agency

General book job websites

bookjobs.org
lynnepalmerinc.com
mediabistro.com

Additional publishing information:

publishers.org Association of American Publishers
literarymarketplace.com Literary Market Place (LMP)
publishersmarketplace.com Sign up for Publishers Lunch here
publishersweekly.com Sign up for Publishers Weekly Daily here
publishingperspectives.com Info on international publishing

Once you get to New York

consumerist.com/2007/01/06/how-to-move-to-new-york-city-sane-and-not-broke
nybits.com
nymag.com/news/features/56013
wnba-books.org
youngtopublishing.com

Additional links throughout book
Preditors & Editors pred-ed.com
Miss Snark misssnark.blogspot.com
BookEnds bookendslitagency.blogspot.com
publishing careers post bookendslitagency.blogspot.com/2010/09/careers-in-publishing-interview.html
on packagers bookendslitagency.blogspot.com/2007/09/what-is-packager.html
Nathan Bransford blog.nathanbransford.com
AIGA "50 Books/50 Covers" aiga.org/about-50-50
Not Always Right notalwaysright.com/tag/bookstore
American Book Producers Association abpaonline.org
Seth Godin sethgodin.typepad.com/seths_blog/2009/06/how-to-be-a-book-packager.html
How Publishing *Really* Works howpublishingreallyworks.blogspot.com/2008/06/how-book-packaging-works_13.html
Publishing Trends of Futures Past www.fresheyesnow.com/shelf-awarenescolumn/publishing-trends-of-futures-past.html
Selective Liberal Arts Consortium slaconsortium.org
Books on the Nightstand booksonthenightstand.com
Publishers Lunch publishersmarketplace.com/lunch/free
Shelf Awareness shelf-awareness.com
Publishers Weekly publishersweekly.com
Literary Market Place literarymarketplace.com
IndieBound indiebound.org/indie-bestsellers
BookPage bookpage.com
Swoon Reads swoonreads.com
Wattpad wattpad.com
YPG youngtopublishing.com/
First Book firstbook.com

About the Author

Carin Siegfried is an independent editor working at her own company, Carin Siegfried Editorial. She has worked as the student assistant to the business manager of the Davidson College library; in customer service at the Vanderbilt University Bookstore in Nashville; and as a bookseller and shipping & receiving supervisor at Bookstar, a regional chain owned by Barnes & Noble. She then went to Ingram Book Group (now Ingram Content Group), the largest American book wholesaler, to work as a junior buyer for the Hearst Group (since sold to HarperCollins) and Henry Holt (a division of Macmillan). Next she moved to New York City and became an editorial assistant at Thomas Dunne Books, an imprint of St. Martin's Press (also a division of Macmillan). During her time there she acquired twenty-six books including a *New York Times* Best Seller and a Barnes & Noble Discover Great New Writers Selection. After St. Martin's, she moved to Charlotte, North Carolina, and got a job at Baker & Taylor, the second-largest American book wholesaler, as an inside sales account manager working with independent stores in the mountains and plains region. She then became the territory manager for New England, traveling to independent bookstores in the region for two years. Next she moved to the national accounts department and began working with Kmart, PetSmart, Petco, and Whole Foods. Since then she has started her own business, Carin Siegfried Editorial, where she edits, crafts proposals and query letters, copyedits, proofreads, writes, consults, and. She also cohosts workshops as Two Editors and a Comma and is an occasional guest speaker. She is the president of the Women's National Book Association.

Originally from Nashville, Tennessee, Carin graduated from Davidson College in Davidson, North Carolina. She lives in Charlotte, North Carolina, with her husband, Jordan, and two cats. Visit her at *carinsiegfried.com*.

Acknowledgments

I would like to thank Libby Westley and Ashley Neff, who have both been incredibly helpful over the years in coordinating my annual talk with the Career Center at Davidson College. I appreciate Kathleen Cook, Sarah Dotts Barley, Melanie Mitzman, and Emily Sachs, and for their expertise and their willingness to share. Thanks to Meg Mendenhall, Leigh Chandler, and Elaine Ruth Boe for providing feedback and asking questions. Thanks also to Quinlan Lee, Jane Kinney-Denning, and Elizabeth Lacks. Karen Alley, Valerie Slade, and Betsy Thorpe provided valuable editorial assistance. Thanks also to Nicole Ayers for her fast copyediting, Kathleen Cook for her razor-sharp and amazingly detailed proofreading, which went above and beyond. And to Tricia Callahan for catching any last errors we all missed in the second proofread and Diana Wade for a fabulous cover and interior design.

"Fun and flirty ... e after page."
—CHR g author

MACY
BECKETT

Surrender to Sultry

❧ A SULTRY SPRINGS NOVEL ❧

ALSO AVAILABLE
FROM MACY BECKETT
AND SOURCEBOOKS CASABLANCA

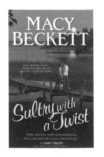
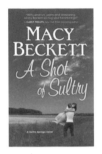

Welcome to Sultry Springs, Texas:

where first loves find second chances...